A Walk by Faith

One Woman's Journey from Domestic Abuse to Spiritual Enlightenment

Dr. Gina L. Myers

Personal Transformation Press
A Division of the Wellness Institute

A Walk by Faith
by Dr. Gina Myers

Published by:
Personal Transformation Press
8300 Rock Springs Road
Penryn, CA 95663
Phone: (916) 663-9178
Fax: (916) 663-0134
Orders only: (800) 655-3846

ISBN: 978-1-891962-32-5

Cover design by Bill Anderson and Tony Stubbs; editing and interior design by Tony Stubbs (www.tjpublish.com)

Printed in the United States of America

For We Walk By Faith, Not by Sight

— Corinthians 5:7

*This book is dedicated to
the thousands of women who are
living in violent situations who don't
believe they have a way out;*

and

*to my Mother who impressed upon
me that a good education is a woman's
freedom!*

Preface

When I reflect upon my past, I am reminded of how far I have come. This horrendous road was my special, private secret. I have been asked to write a book about my experiences because I have been called a "survivor" by many friends.

I believe I am a survivor and I feel really blessed. I have been blessed because I was not murdered. God and my Guardian Angels took good care of me during my dangerous episodes. When I listened to them, they guided me to a better place.

I was rescued by God to fulfill my Divine purpose, which is to help improve the lives of others. I believe I was saved so that I could help others also save themselves. Maybe this little book will help. I pray that it does.

The Holy Spirit will help you reinterpret everything that you perceive as fearful, and teach you that only what is loving is true.

— *A Course In Miracles*

Early Impressions

I was chatting with an old girlfriend and we were catching up on each other's life. When I told her, "I used to live with a violent and abusive husband," she nonchalantly replied, "Girl, if a man ever lays a hand on me, he's outta there!"

Yeah, that seems logical I thought but, from the way she said it, I felt stupid, inadequate and alone. Not having been there, she really didn't have a clue. What did she think of me? That I was so stupid to do such a thing? How could she know what had happened? She couldn't!

I didn't go out of my way to find a dysfunctional, mentally ill, abusive jerk to live with. It was as if my friend thought I **wanted** to be with someone who repeatedly beat me. I took a moment to contemplate the choices I felt I had back then. I didn't recall a line of brilliant and sensitive men standing in front of me, begging me to choose them, yet I just deliberately and intentionally selected a violent thug to begin a wonderful lifetime romance with. No. It didn't happen like that at all. It was not a conscious, deliberate choice. It was an unconscious and unaware choice. My life had made that choice for me, and it wasn't until many years later that I became fully conscious and aware of how it had happened and its fateful impact upon my life. All it takes is one fateful, unmindful choice to shape a destiny. And a destiny without an anchor is of no value.

My story may be very similar to many others. Until I was 12 years old, I lived in the city's Housing Development "projects," and during those early years, I learned about my self-worth, about love, marriage and the importance of getting a good education. From a very young age, I can remember getting a big knot in my stomach after being awakened in the middle of the night by loud shouting and yelling coming from downstairs. Furniture was being pushed noisily around, and things were being thrown. Mom and Dad were fighting again.

There were six kids in my family, and we all slept in one room. We often ran downstairs to see if we could help stop the fighting. Sometimes it worked; they would see all of us lined up on the stairway, frightened, anxious and tearful. I guess the sight of six little kids crying and pleading was enough to quell their violence. They were probably embarrassed by their children seeing their barbaric behavior, incapable of using more peaceful alternatives to resolve their conflicts.

Mom and Dad fought a lot, and it was easy to hear everything in that tiny four-room apartment. They were angry and frustrated, held hostage by circumstances much larger than the both of them. They were married too young, Dad at 20 and Mom at 17. Neither completed college, and Mom had had the six of us by the age of 29 so, of course, she was frustrated. She'd always wanted to go to college, but things hadn't worked out. Her divorced father hadn't fulfilled his part of the divorce agreement, which was to pay for her education so she was brilliant but trapped.

Dad was gifted, too, and really tried hard to stay employed. He worked many different jobs just to earn enough to feed us and pay the rent. When he finally got a well-paying construction site job, it wasn't enough for him. He worried all the time because every Friday, he anticipated being laid off. He really wanted solid work but there were few good jobs for black men in the 1950s, especially if you had no college education.

They fought over money ... or the lack of it. There was never enough for winter boots, coats, food, socks, lunch money, food, underwear, books, food ... you name it, they fought about not having enough of it. They were trapped in a cage of broken promises, shattered commitments, daily frustrations and distant dreams.

Whenever they fought, my stomach would always hurt. When I was seven, I used to sit in a corner and daydream about living with another family, with different parents in a big beautiful house. It was a lovely, gray-painted Victorian house I saw on the way to school every day. I used to stare at that big, beautiful house and daydream about receiving all the loving attention from my parents that I ever wanted. In my dream, I was the only child. I dreamed about having spaghetti for lunch like my classmate Caroline, instead of surplus cheese sandwiches or peanut butter and jelly sandwiches with rock-hard ginger snap cookies. I dreamed about having a nice book bag to carry my books in instead of the green, army surplus backpack we had to wear to keep our posture straight. I was tired of being teased about my backpack!

I was also very tired of being teased about being poor. Folks may talk about growing up poor but they really weren't. I never understood how that could be. All I had to do was look at my classmates and it was pretty obvious to me that our stuff wasn't as nice as theirs.

I felt especially poor at Christmas time. For a long time, we were allowed only one toy for Christmas … and that toy had to come from the Sears catalog. The famous toy catalog arrived in late October and was passed around from kid to kid until everyone had circled the one special toy he or she wanted. When I was nine, the special toy I selected was a Raggedy Ann doll. Dad searched for that Raggedy Ann doll but it was very popular at the time and hard to find. A few days before Christmas, he sat me on his lap and told me he wasn't able to get the doll because the stores were all out of them. I must have looked horribly disappointed because he got up, put on a heavy coat and left the house. I found out later he'd walked all over town in a blizzard looking for my Raggedy Ann doll. He finally found one at the Boston Store, making that my best Christmas present ever.

Raggedy Ann and I were inseparable, and she was a part of me. I dressed and redressed her in the same old dress. I talked to her and protected her when my brothers tried to punch her in the face to get back at me. In fact, for many years, she was my only doll. She was my baby who needed me and I was going to take care of her because she was poor, plain and alone. And nobody seemed to want her.

She was my comfort doll to hold on to during the conflicts at home. While holding "Annie," I discovered what to do when the fights started. I learned how to block it out and pretend it was nothing. I turned my mind off and tuned it out. I went into a daze, a trance, and eventually the daze became a comfortable and safe place to live.

My parents' fights ended as quickly as they started and suddenly they were all cuddly again and making love. Their "make-up" sex bothered me sometimes because I felt that Mom always gave in to Dad too easily, and I didn't understand why. I always wondered why she relented, because she had articulated some really good factual points during the argument. I soon felt myself liking her less for it. From these situations and others, I began to learn that a woman gives up everything, including herself, for her man. He ranks in first place and she is secondary. Men are the Kings, and women exist to serve them. Guys rule!

I also learned that a real, loving relationship is full of regular physical fighting, frequent arguments, and regular passionate sex. If that was marriage, I didn't want any part of it. At the age of 12, I felt that marriage was overrated, and vowed to myself that I would never get married because it didn't seem like a happy situation for a woman.

Also, as early as I could remember, I was receiving regular spankings or whippings. In my view, spankings were much gentler, perhaps using the hand is softer on someone's bottom. Whippings were mean-spirited beatings using a switch, a hanger, a belt or anything else within reach. I really preferred spankings. During rough spells, I used to hide Dad's belt, thinking he'd never find it but he just became angrier while looking for his belt so the whipping was worse. Needless to say, I stopped doing that.

When confronted by Mom about something I might allegedly have done, I would quickly scan the room to make sure there wasn't any type of whipping item within reach. I hated being chastised by Mom when she was ironing because there would be lots of clothes hangers in the room, and she was good at emphasizing her point with a whipping. After a whipping, I'd walk away in tears, feeling like crap for disappointing her. Over time, I grew very anxious and worried about everything that I did. I was working hard to be perfect, to earn their love and approval.

Dad often said I was stubborn and hard-headed because I always wanted to do things my way. I think early on, I was defiant and strong in spirit but my spirit was eventually broken by about the age of eight. I got a lot of whippings for being willful, stubborn and disobedient. It felt as if every time I turned around, I was getting whipped for something—talking back, making up stories (lies) to avoid a whipping, re-doing my hairstyle at school, misbehaving in school, not washing up the correct way, wetting my pants, losing my shoes … the list was endless.

A favorite story my Dad would often tell is about how I would tremble and urinate on myself whenever he called me to ask me if I had done something wrong. I would ask, "Daddy, you gon' whip me?" True, I was very sensitive as a child but I think any kid would have reacted in that way to his booming voice as he yelled and cussed, letting out a quick, fierce and violent temper.

It wasn't until much later that I realized how traumatized I'd been at that young age. I became an extremely sensitive and impressionable girl. Back then, a whippin' was the quick and efficient way to discipline a child but I used to wonder why I got so many whippings, and why my parents would never explain why so that I could learn from them.

Etched in my mind is the time I received my last whipping. I was seventeen years old, and had been accused of something I hadn't done. My brothers had seen me holding the hand of a married man while we were walking around on a Friday night at a summer festival in the park. I'd been told to stay away from this guy and had really tried to, but he was in my Radio Broadcasting class. He was good-looking and made me feel really special. His words were like gold dust on my ears, and no one had ever looked in my eyes the way he did.

When I got home, I went upstairs to my room and fell asleep. I was awakened next morning by both my parents yelling at me at the same time. My innocent pleas were drowned out by their lashes. My mother spat on me and called me a whore. I now understand that they overreacted out of their own private fears. I think they saw in me what they had done at the age of 17, but I was not contemplating a sexual encounter at that time. True, my head was full of romance, music and roses, and holding hands with a man was a big deal for me! But my first sexual encounter wouldn't occur until three years later when I was 20 years old! After that horrible, shameful beating, I remember holding my Raggedy Ann doll and thinking about committing suicide. I felt worthless, shamed and rejected by my parents.

It took me years to fully recover from the shame I seemed to have absorbed from that beating. Now, when I think of all those beatings I received, I understand why my parents disciplined me the way they did, and I eventually forgave them. I now understand where they learned it and what they had learned. I also thought about what they might have been feeling at the time. They were so afraid for me and wanted me to have a better life than they had. I also understand how they were probably limited in their own knowledge and options about how to discipline someone like me. It took me a long, long time to climb out of that deep well of private shame and despair.

I think many Black women and men may have suffered from this mentality of shame from physical abuse. In our culture, getting regular whippings went much deeper than the simple "Spare the rod, spoil the child." I believe it has been ingrained into our culture since the time of slavery, when the "master" would beat us for any small infraction. Whippings have been subconsciously inculcated into our culture, our minds and our ways of being. It is perpetuated in the violence we inflict on each other every day. This practice of harsh discipline is being challenged today. And thank goodness, for it's time for other, more humane, tender and enlightened approaches.

I'm certain that my regular beatings helped sustain my feelings of shame and self-loathing. I remember beginning to feel small inside and withdrawing from that big spirit I had when I first came into this world. This was evident in my first-grade photo, where I was sitting all hunched over. That was around the time I started learning about how to get my parents' approval—through being quiet, helping with the chores around the house, and volunteering to do nice things for Mom and Dad. I felt I would receive their love and affection if I saw to their needs and helped around the house. My Dad would make me massage his back (and he had a huge back). And my Mom wanted me to brush and oil her hair. I hated doing these jobs but this was what they wanted. All the while, I just wanted to be outside playing.

I had a complicated relationship with my Dad. I was Daddy's Little Girl between the ages of seven and eleven, and during these years, I agreed with him, adored him, and worked hard to be physically attractive for him. (My family and relatives were very focused on physical attractiveness.) When I was twelve, I began to feel distant from him because I was becoming my own person, speaking up for myself and sharing my own opinions and thoughts, which often didn't agree with his. He didn't seem to like this, and began to call me "Bones" because of this and because I was very thin. (I was what's called a "late bloomer.")

For several years after that, I was afraid of him. I felt that every encounter with him was harsh, painful and confrontational. I never seemed to do anything right in his eyes. I didn't understand him and he didn't take the time to fully understand me, my thoughts or my desires. Our family was all about him.

To save money, he used to perform all the hair-cutting duties in the house. I remember when he cut all of my hair off. I was 12, almost 13, and wanted to grow my hair longer as I was beginning to feel like a young woman. Well, when I sat down in that chair, I could tell by the way he was holding those clippers that I was not going to get my way.

I pleaded with him not to cut it all off but he kept on clipping and clipping. Through blurry eyes, I saw clumps of my hair falling into my lap and cried when he was finished. At that moment, I felt insignificant, voiceless and powerless. When Mom asked him why he had cut it so short, he said, "It's not too short. It's artistic." What a crock! I hated what he had done but I was trapped in that house and couldn't do anything about it except hate him. Now, I believe he did it to halt my emerging womanhood, to delay my feminine maturity as long as he could.

At the age of 12, I was in a Catholic school, working very hard to fit in but I stood out for three reasons: 1) I was one of the few Black students attending; 2) I wore an "Afro" hairstyle with my navy blue school uniform; and, 3) I wasn't Catholic. By this time, Mom had completed a bachelor's degree in Political Science and had begun working as a Director at a Head Start Program. Life was better thanks to her determination and a kind Caucasian woman (an angel, really) who had given her $1,000 to begin her college education. One day, she just wrote a check for $1,000 and gave it to my Mom, who could hardly believe it! After some serious discussion at home, she enrolled at a local college but it took Dad a while to accept this change.

He had also found steady employment with the electric company by this time. He was the only Black man at the plant and they gave him hell on a daily basis. He seemed to have successfully dealt with whatever ingenious cruelty they could think up. He was smart and courageous in dealing with their petty racist pranks. He didn't drink or smoke, and strangely enough, despite his volatile temper, he never got into any physical fights with his co-workers. To his credit, he was extremely disciplined in matters concerning his job.

With both parents earning decent salaries, we were finally able to move out of the housing projects into a little house with a huge yard. It was only about 10 blocks away, but it was our little Nirvana. An uncle helped us obtain this house and gave us a really good deal. Dad made some great improvements around the house as I watched his pride blossom because we were finally out of the "projects."

While Mom went to school and later worked outside the home, my sister and I took on new duties to help the family. In addition to regular household chores, we did the laundry, planned and cooked meals, monitored the homework completion by our little brothers, went grocery shopping, made dinner menus for the week and ironed about 20 white shirts every Monday afternoon.

Mom ran a "tight ship" and we learned great planning and organizational skills from her. She always reinforced the idea of doing things right the first time. She closely monitored how I completed my chores and provided serious feedback to me. I also learned about how to finish what I started. I felt she was the real person who started the first quality assurance movement, not Dr. W. Edwards Deming.

I was still a very willful, passionate and excited girl, and received much advice directing me to be milder and less assertive. At home, when I got excited about something, my brother would always say, "Tone it down!" so I learned how. I also learned how to win my brothers' acceptance by focusing on their needs. I cooked great meals, served and waited on them, and attempted to look cute and glamorous.

When I started to feel good about myself in my teenage years, my oldest brother began to call me "Dog face," a title that stuck for a long time. It really hurt me and I slowly began to believe that I was unattractive. He later told me he did this to save me from being "stuck-up," but I now think it was because he was having his own problems with his dating partners and I was an easy outlet for his anger and frustration. He was going through his own private adolescent hell.

In spite of these negative messages at home, at school I felt a little more accepted and began to exercise my leadership skills. At the catholic elementary school, I became popular and got involved in a class election for class president. I obtained enough votes for second place and won the vice-presidency. I began to notice my changing emotions towards guys and had a "crush" on a few guys who were very unattainable, yet exciting. I was definitely a Black novelty, but not a romantic, sexy idol like some of the other girls.

At my Catholic high school, I worked hard to get B-grades. It was an all-girls high school, which my parents felt was best for me because there would be no boys around to distract me and my sister. We wore heather blue uniforms, with the standard white Peter Pan collars, wool knee socks, loafers, sweaters, and a blazer (jacket). I hated going to this school and tried to flunk out when I was in the ninth grade, thinking that Mom would be convinced I couldn't handle it.

Mom was no fool, however, and knew me better than I knew myself. She enforced our study hours and provided an algebra tutor for us when we needed one. When I realized I wouldn't win this battle, I started studying more and actually began to enjoy school. I excelled in Spanish, History, and Drama. I really loved Drama and had won awards at competitive events when I was 14 and 15 years old. My special dramatic presentation was from a *Raisin in the Sun* by Lorraine Hansberry, and I loved the poem by Langston Hughes, *A Dream Deferred*:

> *"What happens to a dream deferred?*
> *Does it dry up like a raisin in the sun?*
> *Or fester like a sore, and then run?"*

I hated algebra, and learned to like chemistry and biology. I excelled at school socially and eventually learned how to separate my home life from my school life. While my classmates were dating and going on ski trips, my sister and I begrudgingly were cooking for the family and doing many household chores. I began to enjoy cooking and experimented with pastries, breads, cakes and main dishes. Cooking was very gratifying to me as a creative outlet and gave me a feeling of accomplishment. I also loved how my three teen-aged brothers would always quickly consume everything I had baked, mistakes and all!

I loved walking to school with my sister. We had wonderful conversations and made each other laugh. I admired her because she was smarter than I was and got a lot of A's. Learning just seemed to be easier and more natural for her. We all knew she was going to become a doctor because she loved chemistry and the sciences. We both commiserated about our home life, which was full of structure, oversight and strict discipline. We weren't allowed to date boys until we were 16, and at that age, the Junior Prom was our only date night. What made it worse was that our parents selected the date for us! My sister coped with this strict discipline by reading a lot in her room. She loved romance novels, mysteries, history and *Cosmopolitan* magazine. *Dr. Zhivago* was her favorite book for a long time.

In high school, as in elementary school, I was one of a few Black students who attended the Catholic schools. Being so rare and unusual, I continued to be a social novelty and really enjoyed the attention from it. People were really nice to me and seemed to accept me.

In spite of their penetrating curiosity about Black pride and the race riots, I liked them, too. I patiently entertained their questions about why Blacks were rioting in the big cities, and whether I wanted to be like "Julia." (The character of Julia was played by Diahann Carroll, who represented the first Black woman in a starring role on television who was not a maid or a prostitute.) And, of course, the big question about my Afro hairstyle was, "How do you get your hair like that?"

I tolerated these questions for the most part because many of them were genuine and innocent questions. I felt like an ambassador for the Black race. It was a highly responsible yet tiring position to hold on a daily basis, but I felt it was a small price to pay for being accepted. In providing palatable answers to my Caucasian associates, I had to balance what I shared about the Black Panthers, Malcolm X and Dr. King, without appearing hostile or militant. I had to find a socially acceptable yet truthful response, and that took great skill.

I became adept at raising their consciousness with a little bit of humor thrown in. I learned that my strong, passionate emotions about social issues were a little frightening to them. With humor, I was able to move them towards my perspective more easily. I quickly learned that they were more comfortable (i.e., less threatened) with a little bit of humor whenever we talked of serious social issues.

I thank my Mom and Dad for instilling in me a strong social consciousness. My parents knew only too well what the Black struggle was all about; they lived it each day. In spite of their honesty, superb work ethic, and humanitarian outlook, they experienced discrimination on an almost daily basis. Because they were persistent about having a better life, they suffered a lot of setbacks and disappointments. For example, when they sought better employment and housing, they experienced discrimination.

I'll never forget seeing my mother one day, sitting on the sofa, just plain drunk. She had an empty wine bottle next to her and was crying about not being able to buy a house we all wanted in a great neighborhood. I was shocked to see her like that because she never drank. Her Dad was an alcoholic and she had seen firsthand the results of alcohol abuse. I remember sitting next to her, asking her why she was crying. She just mumbled something about everything being so hard. At this rare moment, she was so sad, vulnerable and disillusioned, and I was sad with her, feeling her sorrow and sensing the fragile side of her spirit for the first time.

She was such a warrior for civil rights that I was stunned to see her like this, because it was not in her character to break down tearfully. She would get angry or frustrated, but rarely tearful. Mom and Dad had to contact the mayor of the city to ask him to intervene, so that we could purchase the house we desired, which was in an all-white neighborhood. My parents stopped at nothing to get what they believed we deserved. My Dad often told me I could do anything in life I wanted to do, and to just have courage and fight for what you want. He told me, "No one is better than we are."

My parents always worked extremely hard to obtain a better way of life for us. Dad performed all kinds of jobs until he obtained steady employment at the electric company. Mom always worked hard to achieve the nearly impossible. She taught my Dad, she taught us, she taught the community about what was possible. She constantly exhausted herself to achieve dreams for everyone. She helped people receive training and entry-level jobs, and was the community's hero. She helped everyone and gave so much of herself to everyone. I've never known anyone who gave as much as my mother, and she was a veritable "superwoman," doing it all. She worked to be a great wife and a great career woman. In her last seven or eight years of life, it seemed to be very important for her to do it all, and even started to do the cooking at home!

Sometimes I was angry or jealous of how much she gave to others outside of our home. I wanted more of her affection and attention, and learned how to get that attention by doing more chores, getting better grades and volunteering to help with the community activities. Everyone knew us because Mom was so well-known in the community. If anyone could do the impossible, she could!

Due to my Mom's involvement in the community, our family was heavily involved in community activities. We helped build playgrounds, cleaned the beaches, painted buildings and helped organize fundraisers.

Keeping engaged in all this activity was a great way to keep our family together, and I learned a lot about "grass roots" activism and social movements. We distributed so many flyers throughout Black neighborhoods that I hope I never have to distribute another flyer in my life. Thank God for email and the Internet!

Mom's Death

My Mom had a nice round, soft figure. Even though she was always twenty or thirty pounds over the ideal weight for her height, she always looked good in her clothes and never worried about her weight. One day when she was about 37, I began to notice she was losing weight and had started to take vitamins. When I asked about these new habits, she began lecturing me about the importance of taking vitamins and convinced me that vitamins were really beneficial rather than just a health symbol.

Later that year, on New Year's Eve 1973, I felt a strange sensation and saw something strange in the house. We were all in the living room near the Christmas tree and I said to Mom and one of my brothers, "I just saw a strange entity in the house, like the Grim Reaper. I've got a feeling that something really bad is going to happen this year."

Mom just looked at me and said nothing. I later learned that she knew she was dying of cancer but chose to not share this information with anyone. Looking back, I don't even think my Dad knew.

In late March 1974, she collapsed in the hallway near the side-door entrance. The ambulance arrived within minutes, and it was surreal to watch the paramedics lift her onto the stretcher. We found out a few days later that the doctors had given her only three weeks to live.

When we visited her in the hospital, she tried to put us at ease and offered us a pack of Lifesavers candy. I jokingly told her. "No, you need it." It was a really bad joke, even for an awkward 17-year-old. Dad just looked at me and shook his head. Before Mom passed away, she wrote and hand-delivered a note to each of us. These death-bed notes were very powerful. Mine read:

> **"Gina, you're a sweet child.**
> **Try not to be selfish.**
> **Baby Poppa, he needs it."**

Three weeks later, on April 17, 1974, she died in the hospital at the age of 39. My Dad was devastated, and it was only the second time I saw him cry. We kids were stunned with disbelief, and for a brief time, we shuffled around the house without looking at each other. Despite it being spring, our big house eventually grew cold.

Two days after she passed away, we were preparing our house for guests who would be arriving after the funeral. I was standing in the hallway where she had collapsed three weeks earlier. I smelled her perfume and was suddenly jolted by her presence. I actually felt her spirit move through my body, an uncomfortable and new sensation.

In the succeeding years, I felt myself becoming more responsible for everyone in the family. I looked after Dad, or "Poppa," making certain his lunches were neatly packed and his dinners were prepared and served on schedule.

I also felt extremely responsible for my three younger brothers, who all seemed to be on their own "trips" after her death. They were young teenagers, handsome, energetic, willful and sensitive, and had frequent clashes with my Dad for breaking his house rules. Some of these arguments became violent and one brother was thrown out of the house for smoking marijuana. He was forced to move into a cold, empty apartment on the other side of town because he had broken one of Dad's rules.

Rule or no rule, it was horrible to see my gifted and sensitive brother being treated like this. He had been the closest to my Mom and, in fact, she had spoiled him a lot because he was so brilliant and athletic. He was also a paranoid schizophrenic, but we did not know this at the time. We just knew that he and Mom had a very special relationship.

We all felt so powerless when Dad kicked him out. We had group discussions to try to change Dad's decisions but it was useless. He didn't listen to us. What he wanted instead from us was constant agreement even when he was blatantly wrong. I still regret not being able to help my brother at this time because I was so fearful of Dad. He became a monster to me and I avoided being near him whenever I could. He was very forceful about his "rules," which I obeyed but on the inside, I hated him. I hated that he wasn't more loving to my younger brothers. I hated that it seemed to be all about him. I hated my life. I hated my Mom for dying.

Dad became mean, bitter, selfish and intolerant, and would frequently tell us how he wished we would all get the hell out of his house. Well, we all eventually did. Few of us ever went back to visit him, especially after he sold our big house and bought a much smaller house for himself. We interpreted this move as a symbol of how much he really didn't want to be bothered by us. To him, it was just a small step towards healing his colossal grief.

After I moved away to college, I never took the opportunity to go back during a summer break. I learned that two of my younger brothers were in and out of trouble. One brother began starting fires and was arrested and jailed. Another moved out of the house due to physical fights with my Dad. I'll keep to myself what I thought of my Dad during these episodes except to tell you that for many years, we all loved to watch the *Andy Griffith Show* and *Family Affair* with Buffy and Jody because we wanted a father like the kids had on those shows. Their fathers were patient, kind, loving and attentive. Once our Mom died, I slowly realized that she had been the long-standing buffer between us and Dad's intolerance and inadequacies. He made us all feel as if we were uninvited guests, like pebbles in his shoes.

Mom made us all live a certain way, and she controlled everything about the family. Once her strong matriarchal hold on the family ended, we no longer had Sunday dinners together, were not forced to attend cultural and educational events together and were no longer galvanized to help the community. We were emotionally and physically separated from her and from each other. Each of us who left town did eventually venture back home for a brief visit with Dad, but it was always short because he became intolerable after a few days.

Granny

The saving grace during many of these childhood years was my grandmother, Sarah. "Granny" as we called her was the best. We loved being at her house during the summer months, helping her in her beauty shop. I admired her independence, hard work, popularity, and loving spirit. I could talk to her about anything. Once, when I was 15, I asked about how I could deal with Dad if I decided to marry a white guy. We used to call him the Black "Archie Bunker" because he never let up on his negatively entrenched view about White people as a collective group.

My grandmother's house was our safe haven, our sanctuary. Often, during my parents' fighting spells, we would be sent to Granny's, and it was great to escape our domestic hell for refuge at her house. There, we could always have second servings of food and had plenty of space to play indoors or outside. We just had to be careful to not step on her flowers or hastas that lined the front yard.

Granny was a fantastic cook, and her Sunday dinners were fabulous! She always made enough for "drop-in" visitors. When each of us took turns to spend a day or a week with her, she would always make our special meal. My favorite was her cheeseburgers with a fried egg, cheddar cheese, and lettuce; I would eat two of them. I loved my "alone time" with Granny and followed her around, watching her do just about everything, especially how she organized her activities for the day. Monday was laundry day and there would be a huge pile of towels to wash for the beauty shop, which was at the other end of the house.

I loved answering her phone and helping her write down the names in the appointment book for hair appointments. I watched her stock supplies, count her money, make orders, and do hair. She was smart and talented, and I learned so much from her. She cooked, sewed, organized, and managed her hair styling business. On Saturday nights, she would often make a dress on her sewing machine for church.

The most important gift I learned from my grandmother was her intolerance of violent and abusive men. I learned that she had endured three husbands, two of whom had been alcoholic and abusive. When I was about seven, I saw how she handled the last one. He had been drinking and was boisterous and rowdy, so she simply locked him out of the house and made sure he never came back. I had heard about another husband's mistreatment towards her. For a long time, she had suffered from his violence but one morning she'd had enough of his behavior. She prepared a nice breakfast for him of grits, which ended up on his face. She just threw all the hot grits at him! He stopped hitting her after that, but they eventually divorced.

My grandmother reminded me of a sweet, gentle rhinoceros in that she was big, swift and able-bodied. And, you did not want her to step on your toe, accidentally. Prince, her little white dog, quickly learned this lesson and knew how to get out of her way really fast. At least six days a week, she worked hard in her beauty shop, standing all day, sometimes for 14 hours at a stretch, washing and styling other women's hair. She was a really good, professional hair stylist and had a lot of steady repeat customers who continued to come to her for generations. She was a true entrepreneur.

I found out that at about age 16, she had run away from home to marry and went to a trade school to learn how to do hair and to get her license. She saved and wrapped dimes to buy her big house, and opened the beauty shop at the back entrance. At the age of 73, she went back to night school to study for her General Education Diploma (GED) and received it about two years later. It was in the local daily newspaper because she was a role model for so many people. She was phenomenal and my true hero.

As a little girl, I would run happily up to her, stretching my arms out wide to reach across her wide behind for a hug and would sink my cheek into that big pillow. She was always happy to see us and she was so affectionate! She always had a delicious "7-up" pound cake or jello dessert waiting for us to devour in the kitchen while she was working in the shop, watching her day-time "stories" on the television. When there were no desserts in the refrigerator, she would give one of us a dollar to go to the corner store to buy Popsicles for all of us! We would drip Popsicle juice down our shirts as we played on the swing set in the backyard.

Granny had a big heart and we really felt her love. When we misbehaved and got a spanking, we really knew we deserved it. She would even explain to us why she was spanking us. The spankings I received from Granny were very rare but always well-deserved. She seemed to understand what we kids were going through in the early days of my parents' fighting. She knew that Dad was volatile and short-tempered, and managed him with an artist's precision. With my grandmother, I felt safe and protected; she was our protector, our advocate.

Granny died two years after my mother died. She was hit by a drunken driver on her way home from church. With her death, I thought I would never know any more happiness. My gentle anchor was gone forever and we only had Dad left to deal with—not a pleasant thought. I was 19 years old and torn between staying home to "take care of Poppa" and escaping to create my own life. I repressed much of my own grief in order to help family members cope with both of these losses. I figured out how to cope by doing, serving and achieving. The pain diminished when I focused on others and did what I felt would make them proud of me.

Higher Education

I had been attending a local college on a campus for two years, and for the third and fourth year, I had the opportunity to go to the main campus in State College, Pennsylvania. I had been doing quite well in college, in spite of my fear of having guys in my class. By this time, I was on the Dean's list, had won some awards and was also spending a great deal of time helping to keep the house running smoothly. I went away to the main campus in "Happy Valley" State College, Pa. and did not return home during the first summer break. I found a job as a waitress at a major restaurant and rented a cute efficiency apartment. Dad was very disappointed when I did not go home that summer.

Having my own place felt good, and I had learned great organizational and planning skills from Mom. I managed to work my way through school with a federal grant for the first year, several school loans and the college work-study program. In spite of a few heart breaks, my perseverance and determination paid off and I finished college in four years, majoring in Spanish literature. The last two years were extremely difficult; especially the Spanish Morphology class.

I tearfully watched my cumulative grade point average drop with each demanding and complex Spanish class, going from a 4.0 to a 2.99. I desperately wanted to major in Theatre but didn't switch majors because I wanted to finish what I had started. My big treat to myself would be a visit to Spain when I obtained my bachelor degree. Choosing to major in Spanish was one of my major moments in which I did not follow *my* heart, *my* passion. I was being the obedient daughter because before her death, Mom had "convinced" me that I was going to major in Spanish, not Theatre. Of course, I didn't argue with her because you rarely won an argument with my mother.

I loved the theatre. I loved being able to "go away" and become someone else. I loved being able to channel my passions and express my strong emotions in a legitimate way. Mom felt that I wouldn't be able to support myself with a degree in Theatre, so out of allegiance and dedication to her, I majored in Spanish literature and minored in Theatre.

When each of us returned home to visit, we would continue to take regular drives around the peninsula to reminisce about how much fun we had at the beach together as a family. After Mom's death, Dad spent a lot of time driving around the beach, full of sorrow. I'll never know how lost and alone he must have felt. He did appear to have some support from his family who lived in the same city, but eventually he became very depressed.

During these times, we questioned God and our faith, and wondered why a loving God would do this to our family. Was it Mom's time to leave us? Had she already completed her mission here on earth? I felt that she had certainly accomplished a lot during her brief 39 years. We all believed she was a workaholic, always working and trying to do it all, to be the Superwoman of the 70s. Maybe death was her final rest. She certainly had earned it.

During hard times, it is easy to become philosophical and spiritual for lack of any other way to rationalize the pain. Back then, we searched hard for spiritual and philosophical answers because we knew we would not find them in religion. Although early on, we were raised as Pentecost, but were not a very religious family, eventually growing away from their rigid interpretations of the Bible and their punishing beliefs about God.

We later joined a Unitarian church and my parents soon discovered that so many of the church's answers were inconsistent with what they believed. My parents held a radical social perspective of the world, which was a typical view held by their intellectual friends in the late 1960s. My parents began questioning everything and, although my Dad remained closest to the Pentecostal doctrine due to his family ties, the rest of us went our own path about ways to worship God.

We kids continued to hold spiritual beliefs but we discontinued the religious practices of tithing and attending church on Sunday. I became disillusioned with religion and with those who said they were Christians. I felt that religion was full of hypocrisy and that Christians were hypocrites. I discovered that those who practiced their religion, or who told me about how much they believed in God, were just talkers. I didn't see any spirituality and goodness in their lives. Ministers were not professional ministers and didn't appear to practice what they preached.

Preachers seemed to perform all of the vices that the Bible admonished. The more I found out about their characters, the more disgusted I became with them. I thought if they were the ones closest to God and served as the biblical interpreters, then it would be best for me to remain faithless, so I had no faith.

The only thing I believed in at that time was Stevie Wonder's music. Beginning in my early teens, he seemed to sincerely communicate what I felt about love, faith, society, and a kind of higher order that we should all strive to attain. His words were the only thing that talked to my soul. They asked me to believe in something, to believe in my divinity. I adored his spirituality because it beckoned me to go further, to continue on.

I needed this encouragement because I often felt hopeless, unworthy, ugly, and stupid. In my quiet moments, I was reminded of how small and incomplete I was. These internal messages began surfacing when I was about 14 and continued dancing in my mind for many years. Keeping active helped me focus on other things, and I have always stayed busy to drown out these messages and gain the approval of others. My activities and achievements helped to cancel out my deep feeling of being inadequate.

When my mother died, I had the opportunity to work even harder, to take care of everyone, to become a hero in her stead. I felt that was what she wanted me to do. Take care of Poppa, keep things together and look after my younger brothers. For several years, I focused on doing these things and forgot about my own sadness and grief. I intentionally postponed my grief. I just repressed it, and didn't have the time for it. My personal mantra was: "Be your own hero," so I decided to be my own hero. I felt that no one was going to save us; we had to do it for ourselves so I continued to work hard to achieve my own dreams and to be of help to my brothers whenever I could.

Spain

In my senior year of college, I began planning a trip to Madrid, Spain, to continue studying Spanish and to perhaps attend the University of Madrid there. Upon graduating in May and after my summer job as a camp counselor, I left for Madrid. My family and relatives gave me a nice "bon voyage" party, and it was a great feeling because I was finally going to get away and achieve my long time dream of working and studying in Spain. I had no plans to come back and dreamed of staying in Spain for the rest of my life. After all those years of studying Spanish, I thought I would finally get a chance to practice the language and really learn it well. I had begun to enjoy living on my own and welcomed any opportunity to obtain more independence.

My wonderful college Spanish teacher, Mrs. Garcia, gave me the name and address of a family with whom I could stay for a few weeks until I found my own place. I had received a warm invitation from this family prior to meeting them in the letters they had written to me. Strangely, when I arrived at their doorstep, I sensed something was wrong. When they told me that there had been a mistake and that I couldn't stay there, I was perplexed. I searched their faces for more words but there was no further explanation. I was just told, "There has been a mistake."

I was told that Europeans were open-minded and accepting, and had not read about racism in Spain during my studying all those years. After a few moments, I finally realized that it was probably my skin color. The family hadn't known I was Black until I had arrived there. When they finally saw me, they were very surprised and awkward. I couldn't think of any other reason for the rejection. I resisted thinking that it was because of my *skin color* and desperately wanted another reason.

Over the next several months in Madrid, I found that racism existed in Spain, too. I learned that Black immigrants from Africa were treated the worst, being denied housing and employment. However, when Madrilenos (people who lived in Madrid) found out I was from America, they seemed friendlier and I felt more accepted. That was my first harsh reality lesson in Madrid.

In looking for a place to stay in Madrid, I found a hostel (dormitory type hotel) where I stayed for a few months. The building was made of stone and very old, and the rooms were sparsely furnished yet spacious, with two large French windows that let in the cold damp air, adding to the indoor chill of the large dark hostel. There was no central heating, just little gas tanks in the bathrooms and kitchens.

I dreaded walking down the hallway each morning to pay my 25 pesetas to the hostel attendant for a hot water shower. Middle-aged, with some rotten teeth, and a chain-smoker, he gave me the creeps. I would always shower quickly because I didn't feel the bathroom was a safe, private place. Sometimes, I didn't care whether the water got warm or not; I wanted to get in and out of there and run back to my room.

Ana Maria, my room mate, was from England and very friendly. When my money started to dwindle before finding a job, I couldn't buy food on a regular basis and had very little to eat, so Ana Maria shared her yogurt, fruit and bread with me for a few days. I hated taking a handout from her but I was hungry. I assured her I would pay her back when I found a job.

I was disgusted with myself. I had planned my venture well for Madrid, or so I thought. My plan had involved attending a language school for three weeks and, when class was finished, I would find a job and live in Madrid. My plans did not work out that smoothly. Each day, when my language class ended, I searched throughout downtown Madrid for a clerical or teaching job, visiting each new office with resume in-hand and newfound humility. The people I encountered were very friendly, but they were not hiring. I started to worry as I was running out of time … and money. I lived on about a dollar a day, subsisting on fruit, yogurt, bread and occasionally a fresh trout or "jamon" Serrano, which was a slow-cured, salty ham.

I felt sad, sick and lonely, and was not having the fun I had dreamed of during all of those years of studying Spanish. The weather in Madrid during October, November and December was bleak and dreary. The air was tainted with heavy cigarette smoke because it seemed everyone smoked. The best part of my stay in Madrid was the food, when I had the money to buy it. It was always fresh and reasonably priced. I loved the fruit, and ate so much during the first few weeks that I eventually became ill with diarrhea. There is nothing worse than having a really bad case of diarrhea, feeling cold all of the time, longing for modern appliances and feeling homesick for your brothers.

No matter how bad it got, though, I was not going to write home for money. I felt this was my great opportunity to be independent and make it on my own. I really wanted to show my father I could make it, that I could do something great! I had longed for this day to prove that, and wanted to be like "That Girl," making it on my own in a big city.

After searching the streets of Madrid for several weeks, I landed a job with a small private language school. My interview with Señor Pardo was a success. I really begged him for a teaching job, telling him I was desperate. He seemed like a kind man who was willing to help a young woman far from home, and I was grateful for the opportunity. I promised to be the best English teacher his school ever had. I was also happy about being able to pay back Ana Maria for the yogurt and fruit she had shared with me.

After meeting his young secretary, Maribel, I learned I would be teaching adult (17 to 60) night school. I worked from 9:00 a.m. until 1:00 p.m., and after the siesta, I worked from 4:00pm until 9:00pm. Siesta time was used to go home for lunch and take a nap. The entire city took a siesta and all of the stores were closed. This custom was new to me and initially it seemed to make my day very long, but once I got used to it, I loved it. I took the time to relax or prepare for my evening classes.

Each day, when I greeted Maribel, we chatted a little. We became friends easily and she began to share the office secrets with me. She would let me know when my schedule was going to change due to official holidays, low student enrollment, or the boss' mood. She also shared the latest scoop on who was interested in me romantically and whether he was a good guy. Many were not. They only wanted to have an experience with a Morenita (i.e., cute brown girl). I appreciated her kindness and caring.

For several days, "el jefe" (the boss) told me how his school needed a photo of me for the file, and requested that I bring one in for the office records. I didn't know where to get a photo made, having looked unsuccessfully for photo shops and corner kiosks. Finally, I just stopped searching, hoping that it would no longer be needed. Then, one morning, Maribel told me that the boss was going to take the photo himself, but warned me to be careful around him. I promised her I would, but wondered why she given me that warning. I was young and naïve, and had no idea what was about to occur.

On the day I was going to have my picture taken, the boss appeared at the office in a very pleasant mood. He was very nice to me and took me to lunch at a unique restaurant where all the staff seemed to know him quite well as the maitre d' directed us to his special table. During lunch, my boss graciously provided a tutorial of the Spanish culture and told me how he wanted to educate me about Spanish history, its people, and especially the foods, the wines and liquors. I was eager to absorb all of it, since I had just spent eight years of studying the language and some of the culture.

We had a wonderful meal, with several courses and several fine liquors and wines with each. With each new sampling, he presented a geography or history lesson about its origins. I learned about a Greek liquor that tasted like anise or licorice. It was served in a small shot glass, to be enjoyed quickly. I asked if I could have another, unaware of the high alcohol content. I lost count of how many liquors I sampled, and when it was time to go, I could barely stand up. I felt embarrassed and foolish for having drunk so much. As we walked back to the office, I kept apologizing for drinking so much but he didn't seem to mind that I was totally smashed!

The brief walk cleared my head a little and when we got back, he gestured for me to go back to his office with him. I was amazed and surprised at the studio setting he had created—professional lighting, a backdrop, and a sofa. He motioned me to sit down on the sofa and I innocently asked him, "Why do you need all these lights and equipment for a photo of my face?"

He said, "I want it done well. Now, hold your head up," and began taking photographs of my face. When he told me to remove my sweater, I obediently did so. He continued taking pictures as he directed me to show him different poses and angles. After he had taken several photos of my face and shoulders, he nonchalantly told me to remove my blouse. Startled, I looked up at him. Still drowsy, I gulped, and then slowly told him, "I can't do that."

He insisted again that I remove my blouse so I sat upright and told him firmly, "I will not do that." With a huge look of disappointment, he began telling me how prudish I was, and how I didn't know how to be a real woman who was comfortable with her body.

In retaliation to his insult, and my wanting to prove I was a real, independent woman, I decided to remove my blouse. I heard a little, gentle voice inside of me say, "This is creepy. This is not right," but I didn't listen. As he continued to take pictures of my tan laced bra and smooth mahogany skin, I began to feel very uncomfortable. When he told me to remove my bra, I gave him a disgusted look and yelled at him, "No!"

I quickly picked up my floral blouse and burgundy sweater, ran out of the room to the bathroom and locked the door. Hoping he would not follow me to the bathroom, I sat there upset and crying for a long time. After my fear dissipated, I began to feel sleazy, like a slut and a whore, and heard all of those condemning voices echoing from my Dad, Mom, and the nuns. Shamefully, I couldn't believe what I had just done.

When I summoned the courage to leave the bathroom, I quietly slipped out and went home, thinking about what had just happened. When I called Maribel to tell her what had happened, she was appalled and told me to be careful because he might fire me. She was right! The next day when I returned to the office for my morning classes, Maribel told me that the schedule had changed and I would only be working in the evenings. We both exchanged knowing looks. The schedule change cut my salary by half, and I knew it was because I had not submitted to the boss' dirty wishes. However, I didn't regret it, realizing I had just had my first lesson about the proverbial "dirty old man." I just knew I had to find another way to make more money to pay my rent.

I explained my money situation to Maribel and she told me about tutoring opportunities at the University of Madrid. At the university, I went to a job announcement board where I found some names and phone numbers of people who needed an English language tutor. I set up two tutoring schedules, one with a widow and another with a lovely family. The widow was a little distant and I liked tutoring the family much better.

This family consisted of a father who was an optometrist, his wife, and their four darling children, a boy and three girls. The children were well-behaved, attentive and smart, and I enjoyed tutoring them. I loved visiting their warm home, full of love, kindness and affection. I longed for each Tuesday so I could be there, right in the middle of that family's warmth. I even daydreamed of living with them as their teacher and nanny, just to feel safe and protected in that strange city.

The incident with my boss encouraged me to think about the kind of lifestyle and career I needed and wanted to have in Madrid. It was very much a male-dominated culture and society, not a progressive city for women. As a woman, I felt repressed and inhibited, and definitely had "my place" in their society. I had just left the United States in 1977, where woman were fighting to be equal to men in their careers and earning power. In Madrid, I felt as if I was stepping back in time. I sensed that a woman's role was to bear children, take care of a husband, and if they dared to dream about having a career, a secretary, teacher, or nurse were to be their highest intended achievement.

Truly daunted, I began to plan how much longer I would stay in Madrid. I knew I wouldn't be able to realize my career dreams in a country that pervasively viewed women as sexual objects and servants. I was eager to return to the U.S. to attend graduate school and continue to realize my ambition. I longed for the freedom I was gaining in the States as a Black woman. And I missed central heating, pristine supermarkets, electrical appliances, my fellow African-Americans, my brothers, my dog Sport and my doctors!

Back in the U.S. of A

When I arrived back in America, I took some time to reconnect with my relatives and my brothers and found out they really were worried about me when I was away. I told them that after all those years of studying the Spanish language, I had to go to the country, that it was something I just had to do. By this time of course, my Spanish was excellent, and my family admired my language ability. Admired as a unique skill, I simply saw my fluency in the language as a definite survival skill while I was away in Madrid.

Living at home was not joyous, for Dad was still grieving Mom's death. He was sullen, mean, and very controlling. I felt I was walking on a tight rope every day. I meekly navigated around his varying moods and temper, my thoughts constantly focused on what I needed to do to get out from under his overbearing, crushing authority. So I diligently worked towards my next career goal and my permanent exit from that house.

While at home, I was lucky enough to find a well-paying job at a local public television station as a freelance scriptwriter. Thankfully, the station manager already knew our family so I didn't have to scrounge around for good references to show him. I was a good writer and, with a little direction, became a good researcher and fact-finder. After struggling with the Spanish language, writing those scripts in English was so deliciously easy. I loved the expressiveness and comfort I had with my native language and did so well as a writer that I was offered a permanent position with a high potential for advancement. However, I turned it down to go to graduate school.

I was really intent on obtaining an advanced degree and felt strongly that my destiny wasn't there at the TV station. Also I didn't want anything that would keep me in my home town. I needed more challenges and I wanted to make much more money. I believed the goal of more advanced education would guarantee a better lifestyle for me in the future. I was glad my parents had taken the time to explain the value of higher education, and that I'd listened to them!

At home, I cooked dinners, did chores, and studied for my Graduate Record Exam (GRE) which would enable me to go to graduate school back at Penn State. I loved studying and began to learn how to overcome my fear of new and difficult subjects. So many technical books are poorly written, and I realized I could break complex things down into smaller pieces and then find other, better-written books to explain an idea. With some time and diligence, I knew I could eventually learn anything.

One of my brothers often teased me about loving books and studying so much, calling me a "professional student." He couldn't understand my love for knowledge and how studying was very gratifying for me. There always seemed to be an immediate return on the investment I put into it. If I studied hard, I would obtain better grades! More importantly, it was one small piece of my world I could control and predict. It was also my escape to a private world of safety, reason and predictable reassurance.

I discovered early on that all of the effort I gave to studying was later compensated for with success, recognition and confidence. Studying for my GRE to enter into graduate school was an example of this. Finally, after all of the studying, when I took that exam, I got a decent score! At my interview with the Department's Chair, he gave me the impression that my score was above average, which felt great. I quickly packed my things and moved back down to the Penn State campus to begin taking classes in the School of Public Administration.

Graduate School

My actual choice of the School of Public Administration was the result of using an unusual decision formula. I really had no idea of what to specialize in and just knew I wanted to obtain a Master's Degree in something. The only things I knew for certain at that time were: 1) I loved providing services to people, and 2) I wanted to learn about management. So, I thought "Public" for working with people, and "Administration" for learning about management. Geeez!

I went back to Penn State because I knew the school, its reputation and location, and I didn't want the added stress of learning about a new school. I just wanted to focus on the books and finish my degree quickly. Since I had very little money saved for tuition, I pursued campus jobs and financial assistance in the form of work-study assistantships. Since I had majored in Spanish and lived in Madrid, I was paid as a tutor to students who were failing their Spanish classes.

For about six months, I also worked at a public television station as a "continuity specialist" between classes. What a boring job! I was the person who researched and described on graph paper the actual times and descriptions for all of the public service announcements, commercials, and any other promotional fillers directed for that specific time slot. There was very little interaction with people, so my primary sense of accomplishment derived from completing each sheet and delivering it to the boss for inclusion in the daily programming.

I left that full-time job because it was boring and allowed very little time for my studying. I needed a lot of study time because the statistics classes were very difficult. As we used to say, "It was kickin' my butt!" Although the teacher was kind, he wasn't very good, and the books were horribly written. So, many times, I found myself combing the campus bookstores looking for easier, better written books to explain regression analysis, analysis of variance, and other warm, fuzzy terms. Somehow I got through those classes but often prayed for myself and for a better breed of basic math and algebra teachers for future generations.

Back then, I didn't pray regularly as I had little to no faith. I often wondered if praying really helped at all because my prayers usually went unanswered. Prayers were merely an empty family ritual to me and I had nothing to back them up with—no feeling, no belief, no testimonial. Sometimes I'd play a daily game of praying in the morning, just to see if there would be a positive difference in my day. Clearly, the days with which I started early with a gentle prayer seemed to flow more smoothly and were better, often much better. It was still just a little mind game I played with myself, while trying to endure that vacant and lost feeling in my soul.

I still wasn't convinced I needed Jesus' presence in my life and I really didn't care to know God at that time. I prided myself in professing that I was a spiritual and moral person and this helped me rationalize and deny my lack of devotion to God. I felt that God probably still liked me some, because I was not doing any harm to anyone, and always tried to do the right thing.

Still, my life was broken and I felt that only I could build a better one. My experience had shown me that I was the only one who could make things happen for me. I couldn't rely on my Dad, my brothers or my relatives. In fact, one of the major reasons I wanted to earn more money was to help my younger brothers with their financial needs. I believed that my Dad, being extremely conservative with his money, was not going to share any of his money with them. My hard work and studying began to pay off and created a meager, but significant, cash flow for me.

During my graduate studies, tutoring classes were going very well. I loved tutoring athletes. They were interesting, funny and unusual to me. They were big, brawny, capable guys who just couldn't seem to grasp the intellectual basics of the Spanish language. I would describe to them that a language is about structure, discipline, and practice because I knew they could understand the idea about practicing something to get better at it. They just didn't care for the foreign language requirement.

I spent extra time helping a special athlete who was charming and handsome. His grades got better as our flirting grew more serious. After great hesitation and guilt, I allowed myself to fall in love with him. I enjoyed his physical gifts—big, dark brown sculpted shoulders, arms, and a posterior to die for. Sexually we were very compatible, and spent great spans of time in bed having glorious, passionate, insatiable sex. I was willing to do almost anything for him and was unrestrained in showing my love; I gave him everything I had.

One day, while walking home from a tutoring session, he pulled out a joint. I knew he smoked marihuana because this was not the first time I saw him smoking one. I had never wanted to try it, and had intentionally stayed away from drugs like a vampire staying away from a crucifix or sunlight! This reaction had been ingrained in me that drugs can cause you to drop out of school and would eventually ruin your life. I had obeyed my parents but now, however, I felt that since I was nearing the end of graduate school, I was on safe ground and could try it. I wanted to see what all the mystery was about.

Well, it was almost a non-event. I could hardly feel anything with the first puff. But, after being well-coached on how to inhale, I slowly started to feel like everything was going to be okay. I had no more worries. The smooth, caressing calmness of it embraced my entire body. I felt supremely happy and quietly confident. While smoking it, I stopped worrying about things—the family, my brothers, money, getting a job, being loved. Finally, I could relax and just float like an autumn leaf falling from a tree. I liked it a lot. Life was very, very good whenever I smoked it.

Our relationship lasted for about a year. It was a very difficult separation for me and I even contemplated suicide because I felt no one would ever love me again. Looking back, I seemed to be so comfortable with the anxiety, high drama, and pain of that relationship that I expected the mistreatment and the disrespect. There was no physical violence then; he just slept around. A lot! He wanted me to accept it and told me I was "Number 1," but his infidelities really hurt. I was supposed to be reassured by that statement. I really thought he would change but he never did. I held on to that passionate, crazy, volatile relationship for a very long time. We argued about his late nights out away from me. We argued about his broken promises and "no shows." We argued about my feelings, and he told me he wasn't moved by my tears. He had no compassion. So, once again, I felt insignificant and worthless.

I believed he had intercourse with a new woman at least once a week … maybe five new women a week, or more. He was all testosterone. I knew he slept around; and I felt I couldn't do anything about it. It never occurred to me to leave him. I was a loyal, dedicated woman, supporting her Black man. Feeling captured by my beliefs, I cried a lot and wrote poems to express my frustration. Often, I would just deny it and block it out. One poem I wrote reads:

"Passion"

We embrace.
I shut out the light of day to concentrate on your warmth and power.
You call out my name.
I twinkle with passion.
And immediately my body is preparing itself for our violent play.
We find our mouths and exchange lingual hello's.
My tongue is enchanted by yours and the conversation takes an upswing.
My hands go skiing up and down the mountains of your back
In the brown sunshine.
We pause, only to become more serious and lost.
My mouth sucks out your vulnerability and nourishes my being.
I deem you to have strength.
Soon your warmth leaves.
Your power is gone.
Daylight welcomes me back into reality as I see you slither
Out the back door.
I am alone.
© 1979 Gina Myers

As usual, whenever I felt powerless, I turned to my books and I just studied harder. My books comforted me and I became numb to the pain. I knew there was no way our relationship would get better, but it was all I had, all I *ever* had. I needed to leave him but couldn't. I was addicted to the sex and his horrible treatment.

Somehow I had learned that this was the way you suffer and endure crap from your man. You give him everything and maybe, maybe, if you wait long enough, he'll give you something back, like a little piece of his heart. Or maybe he'll even change a little. I was such an idealist, a romantic from watching far too many television romances, sexist movies and arguments at home. Yes, real love was a splendid, violent, sexual, painful thing ... and I believed this without question.

Washington D.C. Internship

During my last year of graduate school, I became aware of an internship program in the federal government for students who were majoring in Public Administration. I was anxious to find a good career opportunity and this one entailed rapid advancement and good pay. I had the qualifications so I applied to the program, endured the rigorous selection process and was selected. It was great having a good school like the Penn State sponsor me and others, and it was great to land an exciting and good paying job. I was overjoyed! My one other job offer was on the West Coast, working as an underwriter for an insurance company, which did not appeal to me at all. I went with the internship because I was still an idealist and believed in the dignity of public service and helping people.

During my internship, I worked hard, learned a lot, and out of my loneliness, made many friends. I did not associate with many of the other interns because I felt they were phony and pretentious. Looking back on this, maybe I just didn't feel comfortable or worthy when I was around them due to my own insecurities. They all seemed to be so much brighter than I was and I felt different, even odd, around them.

The internship was a two-year program, located in the exciting city of Washington, D.C. I was eager to go there and actually see for the first time the Capitol building, the monuments, and the White House. It would be better than seeing it all on television. And I just knew I would have a chance meeting with a handsome, young senator and he'd ask me to lunch! Then we'd date for a while, drive around the city in his convertible, get married, have a wonderful wedding and live happily ever after!

In between my silly daydreams, I realized I had to find an affordable place to live. My sister-in-law gave me the phone number of her brother-in-law who owned some apartments in the area. I was very grateful for this rare connection until I saw the ugly, rundown apartments. They were horrible ghetto-like structures with no grass in front but only barren soil. Disappointed and saddened, I continued searching for a place to live.

A few weeks later, a college school buddy told me about a house her friends owned in Anacostia, saying they probably had an extra bedroom I could rent. I followed up with her referral, talked with the owners and moved in. It was a big old Victorian-style house with three older guys, all Vietnam veterans. Although they were very kind to me, I didn't feel comfortable staying there. They had sloppy habits and the location in southeast D.C. seemed foreign and scary to me.

I felt strangely out of place in Anacostia even though I was among my own race. When I jogged daily at the nearby park, guys on the street jeered and harassed me. I was meek and unassertive, and didn't know how to make them stop, or whether I even could make them stop. Everyone, mostly the men, seemed aggressive, macho and eager to meet me. There seemed to be a vicious sophistication in everyone I met. They seemed to focus on different things and they were always a few steps ahead of me. I knew I was "out of my element," and not streetwise enough, having spent most of my life in school and in a small city in Pennsylvania.

When I told a nurturing lady at work what I was enduring, she said, "You need to get over here on the other side of the river." After several similar conversations with different employees in the office, I learned about the good and bad parts of Washington, D.C. After a three-week search, I got a tip about an available place on Capitol Hill, a cute English basement apartment near Union Station. It was affordable, convenient and small. For a moment, I found solace in a place of my own. However, as the days passed in my apartment, I soon felt lonely and ached for companionship. I came from a large, loud family and missed the noise and activity. I was lonely and needed someone to be with. At the time, I was incapable of appreciating my solitude.

The most challenging part of my internship was trying to understand the social and political culture of a big city like Washington, D.C. I was under-challenged during my internship and often scrounged around for more challenging work, volunteered for new projects and requested to be involved with exciting assignments. I visited my supervisor or other folks in the office to ask for more assignments or more challenging work. Some times my initiative won a good response; at other times, I was ignored. I felt like an ornament and not an integral part of the office's activities.

In the evenings, I had plenty of curiosity and reserved energy for an exciting social life. I often felt like Gomer Pyle in New York City. Easy prey. I was naïve, endearing and easily approachable, especially by thugs and street people. Wanting to be liked, I loaned money to too many people, hung out with office mates who seemed content to just live for the weekends, and dated a weird assortment of guys.

My standards were quite low and I always fell for the cute, charming "flash and dash" type guys. I didn't know what to look for in a man and would settle for anyone who made me feel pretty, who was attentive and who exuded machismo. My weekends were full of nightclubs, cocktails, a regular "joint" and finding a steady boyfriend to help legitimize my strong sexual appetite. The freedom I enjoyed from living on my own and earning a salary was intoxicating. There was always a new adventure right around the corner, especially in the summer! I hated to be at home, alone in my apartment.

The Scarred Lady

One day, while walking home from work, just before getting on the Metro subway, I noticed an older Black woman approaching me, as we both were walking on the same side of the sidewalk. As she grew closer, I suddenly noticed her face, which was horribly scarred and disfigured. She appeared as if she had been physically beaten every day of her life. I was startled by her face, so full of sadness and resignation. It seemed that her spiritual light had departed a long time ago.

She glanced at me and then really looked at me, as if she knew me. I searched her face, feeling pity for her and wondering how often and how long she had endured that kind of life. She seemed resigned to be no more than what she was, whatever that was. I vowed to myself that I would never let someone beat me like that and disfigure my face like hers. I just wouldn't tolerate any of that. Who wants to be scarred like that?

The vision of the beaten and scarred lady stayed with me for a long time. I was intrigued with how a woman could stay in that type of a situation. I thought about how I was different from that lady and knew I would never be in a situation like that. I was smarter, stronger and more capable than she probably was. I challenged myself to dismiss the picture of her face but it stayed with me. Unfortunately, the image of her face had found a resting place in me.

Lack of Awareness

A co-worker in my office, who eventually became a mentor to me, described to me how I was different and that I had a lot of potential. He described how I needed to apply myself and search for deeper meanings to events in life. He felt I was missing out on life because I was not being authentic. I didn't know what he was talking about. He went on to explain how he had recognized that I was kind of "in a fog" and that I never seemed to be living "in the moment," He had noted that I was always reacting to a situation in a delayed manner or was very defensive about feedback and comments toward me.

He was right. What I couldn't control, I wasn't interested in. I had anxieties and fears that seemed to prevent me from reaching a higher place of calmness and trust. His conversations seemed really strange to me, but they were also intriguing so I listened intently. His name was Hagerty, and he was wise, kind, and patient. He told me I didn't need to be a perfectionist, and to not always be so hard on myself. He mentioned a group that helped people "be in the moment" and get the most out of life. He convinced me to attend this "group counseling" session for a weekend. Later, I realized that Hagerty was one of those "angel" friends sent to help and guide you.

Attending this session was the first step in my self-awareness. I became aware of how each individual person is raised very differently in a different family environment full of its own dysfunctional rules and unique values that often contribute to twisted destinies. I wasn't yet aware that I was one of those people. My fundamental psychological problems were much, much deeper but at that time, while still deep in my own denial, I could only have sympathy and compassion for the many others who were probably raised by mean, incapable, or uncaring parents. I still wasn't aware that I had been similarly affected.

I had a lot of compassion for others. As an empathic person, I probably had too much sympathy and compassion for people. I was a care-giver, a rescuer. As a young woman, I wanted to nurture and fix whoever and whatever appeared to be broken for I had learned very early from my parents that by helping others, I would be loved. This was especially true with men and I was kind, loving, attentive and caring towards a lot of men who really didn't deserve it. With these men, I was unable to say, "No," or stand-up for myself. I only knew about pleasing others and addressing the needs of others. It was what I had learned and who I was. I was strangely independent and ambitious, yet foolishly generous and often selfless. I felt happy and complete only when I could focus on others' needs, with my own value reflected only in someone else's eyes, not in my own eyes.

A Taste of Independence

I loved my small English basement apartment on Acker Place, in the northeast section of Washington, D.C. It was a one-bedroom, renovated basement apartment with a walk-out door that led to the alley behind the house. It was a dark, nearly subterranean apartment, though, so I couldn't have any plants due to the lack of sunlight. And it was often cold during the winters because of the sparse but expensive electric heating. I could have been warmer but would have had to pay more for electricity.

I was on a very strict budget, with little left for luxuries or fun. After I paid the rent, utilities and transportation, I could hardly splurge on anything. One day, I did splurge on a boxed pastry from the supermarket. It was so good, stale but good to me at the time. In spite of my budgetary issues, I really loved my little neat apartment because it was all mine. No roommates, loud uncontrollable noises or chatter. It was quiet. Very quiet. Unnervingly quiet. And I often felt lonely.

I had grown up in a large, loud-talking, animated family, reminiscent of an Italian family where all talk at the same time. I missed that noise. I missed my brothers' teasing and my sister's laughter and courage. I hadn't yet developed the ability to enjoy my own company, to relish the solitude and solace of my own spirit. I really needed to be around people. I needed to be with someone … anyone.

This loneliness disappeared at work and I really looked forward to each workday because I could broaden my chances to meet that "special someone" who would warm my heart and fill me up with happiness. I was even eager to hear the shallow lunchtime conversations of my colleagues since it felt just a little like home.

After a few months, I'd learned the work routine of a big city like Washington. I took the Metro each day and learned to never make direct eye contact with strangers for fear of encouraging an unwanted human connection. I learned how to walk down the street with an air of indifference and aloofness. I really began to feel in charge of my life, independent and on my way to greatness. I felt in control of my life and that I was doing everything right to achieve success. I believed that the more I accomplished, the more I would be viewed as a great, successful and worthy person.

I presented a very capable exterior despite feeling inside like an ugly, inadequate loser. No matter how hard I tried, I just didn't match up to the women on the covers of popular magazines or on television. My brothers had always compared me to these women and I'd always lost. I kept trying to be beautiful and would buy the right clothes, make-up, shoes and accessories, but it was useless. I wasn't quite the "brick house." I needed to feel complete and whole, and believed that only through a romantic and loving relationship would I be granted such a wonderful and complete feeling.

Finding True Love

When I met Doug, it was love at first sight. One afternoon, I was walking home from the grocery store, wearing fashionable boots and tight-fitting jeans, and felt I was being watched. I walked faster and faster, only to be intercepted by a small Black man with gorgeous dark eyes and a full beard just like my Dad's.

He seemed to take command of the situation immediately. I was flattered by this direct, aggressive attention. I don't recall his opening line, but just that we began a wonderful conversation full of humor and flirtation. There was instant attraction. He was charming and streetwise, and seemed to know a lot about the city and how people managed to make money on the streets of D.C.

I was fascinated with his stories about the streets, unusual people, con artists and criminals that were fascinating and scary at the same time. I was intrigued because I knew nothing of which he spoke, and he was opening up a whole new world of learning, a world I had missed because I was doing homework and couldn't play outside with the other kids.

We dated for a while and after a few months, we really grew in love ... or so it seemed. I loved the attention he showered on me, the flowers, the drinks, the groceries and the fashionable clothes. In addition to the physical attraction and the great sex, we believed we were perfect for each other. He was attentive, exciting, sexual and commanding. I loved his forcefulness and was easily molded and responsive to his every need. We saw everything the same way and never argued or fought. Everything was smooth and pleasant, and he became my whole world. He called me "Sweetness" and I had several nick names for him. It was just perfect, dreamy, calm and protective.

He was very impressed with my education and my accomplishments because he had only received a high school GED. He had not accomplished much with his own life due to the hardships inflicted by the "White Supremacy" or "the Man." He told me how he frequently had tried to keep a job and that presently he was "in-between" jobs. This did not seem strange to me for I totally understood his situation, recalling how hard it was for my own father to find steady work when we were little kids growing up in the projects. I understood how a Black man in this society could have difficulties.

Doug told me he had served some jail time for drug dealing, which was okay because from his point of view, as a Black man, rules were broken to survive. I didn't judge him negatively. Instead, I loved him and understood how easily this could have happened. I forgave this transgression as well, because I had a brother who had been sent to jail recently. I felt Doug was no worse than my own brother and, in fact, it helped me absolve some of the helplessness I had felt towards my brother's incarceration and towards my mother's death. Meeting and loving Doug helped me tie together those painful loose ends of my life.

Loving him also helped me ease the searing pain from not being able to free my own brother from prison. Somehow I felt that loving Doug would ease my brother's pain as he sat in jail. Loving Doug helped me complete the warm and happy ending of how my Mom and Dad should have lived together in harmony for the remainder of their lives. I thought that perhaps I could help complete the happy ending that never occurred for them.

How I wanted to help him. I just knew and believed that with the "right" woman beside him, Doug could conquer anything! But until then, he had just not met the "right" Black woman. He needed me because I *was* the right woman for him and I was a natural helper. I believed a woman, especially a Black woman, needed to be there for her man to help him grow, flourish and overcome society's obstacles. At the time, I believed that Black men had a difficult life, either unjustly put in jail, were accidental drug addicts, or were always unfairly judged as unemployable.

I was determined not to let this Black man fail. Not this one. I promised I would do everything I could to help him succeed. He promised to love me and to stay with me forever and ever. I would help him find jobs, get his broken tooth repaired, and buy him some professional-looking clothes. I believed that he would excel through my supportive and nurturing attention. I believed I could love him enough so he would want to do more with his life. With the right supportive woman, he'd have no choice but to be great, and we could do wondrous things together!

What a match we were! With the great sex, we naturally fell into a rapture and passion that was so perfect, so strong and so familiar. We really loved and needed each other. Our unknown co-dependence was masked as finding our "once in a lifetime," true, romantic love! Doug was my fantasy come to life. I subconsciously wanted to "rescue" him from his aimless, low life in order to vividly create my real life fantasy of romantic love and happy endings. Doug eagerly enmeshed his needs into my dreams. He needed to be loved and adored as much as I needed to fulfill my romantic story.

Happily in Love!

Doug spent his days looking for work and I spent my days at the office. Each morning when I was selecting my outfit for the day, he would critique each outfit. He was the only one who knew what I really looked good in. He didn't want me to look like a whore. He disapproved of anything that appeared to reveal my curves or physical attributes, and began to buy many of my clothes. I didn't mind this because he bought really nice garments for me. Whenever I asked him where he bought it, he'd say a friend gave it to him. I didn't question him any further and just thought how generous and kind his friends were.

Each day, he would call me at work frequently and occasionally met me for lunch. He was very interested in how I spent my day and when I would be leaving work. He wanted to know about all of my friends and began to criticize each of them for some attribute or action. Eventually he began to tell me which friends were not good for me and how I should stop being friends with her (I didn't have any male friends at the time). He always found something negative about each of my friends and didn't seem to care for any of them. I listened to his advice because I felt he knew better than

I did due to his street wisdom. And most of all, I wanted to please him.

I was obsessively in love, and my thoughts about him were obsessive. I worried each day that no danger would come to him and what I would do if he were no longer a part of my life. I was always thinking of him and would scribble his name on note pads and magazine covers. I thought about new ways to make him happy. For example, when I traveled, I would bring back souvenirs and gifts for him, and often bought greeting cards for him expressing my love. I anticipated his wishes and quickly responded to his requests. I even paid for his dental work. I was often jealous of how he looked at other women and was desperately afraid of him leaving me.

During the week, I worked very hard at my job, made dinner in the evenings, and worried each day about how he was progressing at his newly found job. On average, he kept a job for about three months, often walking away from a job because his boss or co-worker would make him angry. He seemed so confident and eager to work at odd jobs such as carpentry or construction, so I didn't understand why this was happening. He was a good talker and always working on that next big project or that next great "connection." I believed in him and what he told me, never, ever doubting his words.

Like a deer in headlights, I was amazed and impressed with the people he knew from different walks of life. He was so worldly yet I was perplexed by how he didn't seem to grasp basic activities like planning, organizing and paying bills. He understood the streets and opened my eyes to the seedy, limitless debauchery of humankind. I was intrigued with how some people lived and went about their lives, consistently making wrong or uninformed decisions. I was still unaware of how I fitted in this mold, too.

Doug had been living with his mother but moved in with me and advised me that we needed to relocate to get away from the noise and activity of the city. He told me we needed more space and that living in Silver Spring, MD would be good for us. His mother lived about two blocks away from us, and I wondered if, perhaps, he wanted to move further away from her.

Deep inside, I knew that allowing Doug to settle in with me was the wrong decision. However, I couldn't speak up about it. I was unassertive and incapable of disagreeing with him. I had always been easily dominated by strong men and knew that my opinion didn't count for much, so standing up for myself at that time was clearly out of the question. It wasn't even a remote thought, for I would always acquiesce.

By about nine months into the relationship, Doug was dictating to me what I should be wearing, how I should cook and clean the apartment, what friends I should have, and when he was going to pick me up from work with my vehicle. Strangely, I enjoyed this attention and felt cared for and deeply loved. I had longed for a deep, intensely loving relationship like this for most of my life, an all-consuming, devoted love that song writers sing about. This was just what I'd been living for.

Isolation

In the spring of 1982, after some apartment hunting in Silver Spring, Maryland, we found a spacious one bedroom apartment with parquet floors and large bay windows. It was a fine apartment near a Metro station and lovely parks and playgrounds. We moved in and purchased beautiful wicker furniture, gorgeous rugs and wall hangings. My best friend Eva visited several times and commented on how she adored the furnishings and style. Eva was a good friend, originally from New York City, and moved to D.C. for a better secretarial job. We had double-dated and partied together before I had met Doug.

During this second year of our relationship, things seemed to be going pretty well at the Silver Spring apartment. I kept it neat and clean, and enjoyed cooking meals for Doug. Although the relationship felt stable, I was starting to see him less and less as he was rarely with me. Often, on weekday mornings, I had to remove last night's dinner from the oven and throw it away. On weekends, each Saturday morning, he'd awaken, get dressed, roll some joints, leaving one for me as he exclaimed, "I got some business to take care of." With a loud jingle of his keys, he'd be gone. I hated that sound of his keys. Sometimes I'd cry at the lingering jingling sound in my head. I was alone again.

His "business" took all day. He would often be away until 2 or 3 a.m. I had no idea what he might be doing. I was mystified by his absence and wondered if he was with another woman. I thought he loved me and wanted to be with me always and forever. His absence dissolved my dreams of being together to do fun activities such as visiting museums, theme parks or gardens during the day in the Washington area. I wanted to be like other couples who seemed to enjoy visiting all of the wonderful sites together!

When I pleaded with him to stay or when I mildly complained about his absence, he would stay out all night and return that following Sunday morning, so I stopped complaining about my Saturday loneliness. I began to quietly muffle my protest with a long hit from a newly rolled marijuana joint. Once mellow and oblivious, I soon forgot about his absence, my deep sadness and our disintegrating relationship.

Each time I tried to mildly assert my opinion or make known my opinion of the situation, he would become angry. He would tell me, "You don't know what you're talking about. You just need to mind your own business." Then, he'd call me nosey, stupid and lazy. Whenever I questioned his actions, he would say I was preventing him from making money. That I was nagging him and acting like a bitch.

Each day he would drop me off at work and pick me up at the end of the day. He was always at least an hour late. When I complained once about his tardiness, he yelled at me and accused me of giving him a hard time. He knew how to turn everything around and pin the blame on me. Everything was my fault and I believed it. I tried to be better and not complain. I didn't want to make him angry, and just wanted to be as supportive as possible.

What he did during the day remained a complete mystery to me, but he never had any money left. After a while, I knew he was not looking for work because he was always asking me for five dollars. Always just five dollars. I rarely had the extra money because I was paying all the bills and had often given him my last dollar. I soon began to hide money. I didn't know then, but at that time he was using cocaine and PCP. Cocaine provided his calming, euphoric state and PCP was a highly hallucinogenic drug.

I was still trying to be Superwoman, paying the bills, working each day, keeping the apartment clean and cooking the meals. I still believed I could control everything and that our success or failure was in my hands. I knew I had the power to improve the situation and didn't believe in a higher power helping me. I rarely prayed and had faith only in myself at the time. I was quickly losing faith in Doug as he never kept his word. His many promises to me were quickly broken and I couldn't rely on him to help with the bills or the household chores. The situation was not good.

The First Time

One Friday afternoon, I waited and waited for Doug to pick me up from work. Finally, I became fed up with waiting for him. I felt humiliated and stupid for waiting so long for him. With a long sigh, I took the Metro home instead of continuing to wait for him. When I arrived home, I filled the tub for a hot bubble bath. I was feeling so good about how I'd taken a big, courageous step to take care of myself and had demonstrated some control over my own life. I was feeling defiant and independent, keenly proud of how I had just come home on my own without him. I smiled to myself as I slowly sank down into the warm, sudsy bath water, relaxed and feeling complete as the nurturing bubbles hugged and congratulated me.

Those blissful moments abruptly ended with the shaking and agitated sound of his keys at the door. I knew he'd be angry but I felt I could handle it this time. I felt ready to challenge him with words. I tensed up a little, waiting for his harsh, loud words. But there were no words. In a blur of activity, I felt an intense sharp pain in my head as he fiercely yanked my hair with one clenched fist, repeatedly. The quick sharpness and power of his escalated anger stunned me.

Frightened, I dared not look into his eyes. I looked only in his general direction, my eyes glazing over with disbelief and fear. As he continued to blast me with names and expletives, I slowly, cautiously gazed up at him, trying to recognize this person in front of me. The eyes that looked back at me were so full of rage and murder that I quickly looked away. Finally, he snarled, "Don't you ever leave like that," and suddenly left the apartment.

I sat stunned in the tub for a long, long time. The water turned icy cold but I didn't notice because my mind was stretching to wrap a meaning around what had just occurred. I began to realize that it was my fault because I had made him angry. I remembered how much he loved me and struggled to figure out new ways to keep him happy. I realized this behavior was just a manifestation of his deep, true love for me, and I consoled myself by remembering how my parents fought bitterly yet still loved each other. Although this was a new and scary feeling for me, I felt it was going to be okay because I decided I was not going to make him angry again.

I rationalized in my mind how deep love is filled with deep anger. I was determined to not fail in this relationship. I was going to do everything I could do to make this relationship succeed. I never failed at anything. I knew I could do better. I understood how frustrated and distraught he must have been trying to find a good job, trying to keep his pride intact. I was not going to be his enemy. He'd had enough enemies in his life. Through thick and thin, I would have to prove how much I loved him.

I spent that weekend washing my hair, doing laundry, watching children's TV shows (Peewee Herman) and talking on the phone to Terry, who was dating one of his brothers. I described to her how

Doug had yanked my hair, and she sympathized with me while, at the same time, shrugging it off as though I'd told her about a clogged drain. She instructed me about how men are with their emotions, how they don't really mean to hurt us and how much Doug loved me. It was good to be reassured like that.

Doug returned to the apartment on Sunday morning. He brought flowers and a pretty blouse for me. He apologized for hurting me and told me how much he loved me. He always called me "sweet-ness." He made wonderful love to me and promised he would never ever hurt me like that again. He cooked Sunday brunch for us and was very, very affectionate towards me for the next several days. I fell more deeply in love with him, unaware that it would happen again.

Career Woman

$\mathcal{I}$ continued to go to work with flawless attendance, determined to fulfill my career goals. At the end of my two-year internship at a federal agency, I received a Reduction-in-Force (RIF) separation notice. I was going to be laid off because of my short time in the federal government ... thanks to President Ronald Reagan. I felt unwanted, tricked and betrayed. I was a presidential management intern and I thought I was immune from the regular bad luck of normal working people. When this denial wore-off, I began searching in the private sector for an interesting and decent paying job. However, I soon learned that Public Administration does not transfer well to the private sector. The leads I had received did not result in job offers. Public Administration was for public service and truthfully, I really wanted to stay in the federal government.

I was fortunate, well, sort of. As a result of the networking of my internship mentor, I received a new work assignment at the Depart-ment of the Navy, working at a research lab. Even though I had to take a demotion, I was really very happy to be employed. Secretly, I knew I would "wow" them and get my original pay grade back. I was smart, inventive, hardworking and enthusiastic, and the job suited my skills and talents perfectly. I became a workaholic. The harder I worked, the more easily I could forget about my troubles at home. My job was also the one thing in which I felt I could easily exert control.

As a program specialist, I worked very long hours to help me forget about how my relationship with Doug was changing. He was still arriving hours later to pick me up from my office building, which was far from the city, in a semi-rural setting. I would wait on the steps of the building for hours and watch everyone else depart for home. I felt humiliated and powerless. When people asked me about his tardiness, I pretended that it was really okay.

On occasion, I would speculate how late he was probably going to be and stay in the office, working until that specific time. It was less humiliating to do it that way for no one would see me waiting for hours on the steps. That plan was discontinued when I once arrived at the steps later than he did. I had to silently endure his wrath, verbal abuse and reckless driving all the way home. Sadly, his behavior wasn't about being fair but about power and domination. I was supposed to wait for him but he was never, ever supposed to wait for me.

Doug was changing. Regularly, while driving home from work, he would ask for five dollars. When I would tell him I'd given him my last five dollars, he would become very angry and agitated, and start driving very fast and recklessly on the road, barely avoiding accidents, and sometimes not avoiding accidents. He had frequent accidents and it was always the other person's fault. I began to hate riding with him.

Each day, he would drop me off at home and keep going. I stopped asking him where he was going, because his response was always: "None of your business. Stop being so nosey." During this time, while working at the Department of the Navy, I had only three pairs of shoes and a modest wardrobe because our money just seemed to disappear far too quickly. I began to misplace or lose items around the house, only later to find out that he had taken them to exchange for drugs. I began to withdraw at home and started to blankly stare out of the window more than I'd like to admit. I began to think he was not the guy for me but had no idea about how to finesse a peaceful separation.

One day when I returned from the grocery store, I noticed Doug standing in front of the dining room table, jeering at the mountain of marijuana he had just obtained to sell. I stopped and stared at the huge mountain of "grass" that nearly covered our small dinette table. In disbelief, I asked, "What the hell is this doing in here?"

He said, "I'm going to sell it, and we'll make a lot of money!"

Angrily, I told him, "Get it out of here or I'm leaving you. There are three things I won't tolerate. Selling drugs, cheating on me and hitting me. Nothing is going to mess up my job situation and my career."

To this day, I don't know where that strength and courage came from to assertively express myself with him. He glared back at me for a long time in disbelief; and then slowly began to wrap up the marijuana. I felt relieved and surprised that he had followed my direction! I was even more surprised at myself for chastising him. I began to garner new hope about my possible influence in our relationship. I felt I was beginning to regain some control over my own life, which had been slowly slipping away due to his mean, overbearing and dominating style.

That night, I fell asleep with a gentle calmness that was long overdue, only to be awakened and startled at 3 a.m. by angry shouts from Doug. He called me a bitch, a demon, slut and other creative terms as he slapped me repeatedly and attempted to strangle me. As he pressed down on my throat, I felt the calm darkness envelope me. It grew quiet and peaceful. I seemed to not mind going to another place to escape his rage. Just as I went away, I came back, opening my eyes to meet his murderous eyes. He had let go. I jumped out of bed, gasping and crying, heading for the telephone. He whispered, "If you try to call the police, I'm going to kill you." I stopped, frightened and uncertain about what was going to happen next.

I went into the bathroom to look at my lip in the mirror; it was bleeding. Dazed and feeling hopeless, I tended to my lip with a cold wash cloth. Incredibly, I heard some muffled sobbing from the bedroom. When I entered the bedroom, I saw him sitting on the side of the bed with his head hanging down, sobbing. My heart melted. He cried about how he didn't deserve me and how I was too good and deserved someone better.

I wished I'd listened to him because he was right. But, instead of agreeing with him, I held him and cried with him. I told him how much I loved him and that he needed to get some serious counseling. I assured him we would work on this together and that there was nothing to be ashamed of. He promised he would get some counseling and I was hopeful and encouraged about improving our relationship.

Strangely, he immediately wanted to have sex but I was not in the mood. (Being nearly strangled can affect you like that.) Ignoring my objections, he mounted me and began thrusting. I just tuned out and thought about what I was going to fix for Sunday dinner. I was beginning to hate our sexual relations because I had no say in the matter about when or how we engaged in sex. He wanted it when he wanted it. Basic, forceful and crude. No foreplay. It hurt and I would often just lie there, wondering if this was all there was to life. Wondering whether this was what I deserved because I wasn't beautiful. I thought about how nice it would be to kiss for a long time. What happened to all the passionate kissing that was supposed to occur? I figured it was just on television and in romance novels, and wasn't something I would ever receive. I could count the times on one hand when I'd been kissed on the lips.

Just Don't Make Him Angry!

I got a little wiser and began watching Doug more closely, vigilant and sensitive to any tension, his changing moods and irritations. Everything had to be perfect or else he would get angry and crazy so I tried to be perfect to not make him angry. The house was clean, dinner was on time, and I stopped complaining about his habits. I had researched counseling but he decided to not attend the sessions, saying he felt he didn't need it and that I was the problem. To him, I was lazy, ugly, stupid and a slut who was cheating on him. I had no idea why he was accusing me of all these horrible things.

I attempted to confide in his mother, since my Dad and I were not speaking at the time. She listened and told Doug that any time you point your finger at someone and accuse them of wrongdoing, three other fingers are pointing back at you. I was looking for a little stronger reprimand but that was it. Nothing more. I wanted her to be on my side, to be my mother and protect me from him but I got very little consolation from her. I guess she was trying to survive herself so it really wasn't a big deal at all to her.

One Easter Sunday, when she came over for dinner, Doug had just beaten me the night before and I had a busted lip. I forget my alleged sin—probably because I ate dinner without him or that I'd smiled at one of his friends. When she saw my busted lip, she looked pitifully at me and pulled out her Bible to quote a verse to me. I was amazed and discouraged by her indifference and denial about her son's serious problem. I later learned that she and Doug had shared some violent exchanges and she was afraid of him. One evening, I found out why.

Doug had dropped me off at his mother's house one Friday night and I took the opportunity to have a candid discussion with her. I told her about the increasingly frequent violence and verbal abuse, and that I was going to leave him if things didn't get better. She looked at me blankly and told me, "Stay with him. You're good for Doug. And I'm so grateful about how you paid for his dental work to fix his front tooth and enrolled him in some classes. I want you in his life."

When Doug returned after several hours to take me home, she approached him and gently asked why he had been treating me so badly. He looked at her with surprise and then defiantly began to deny any wrongdoing. He started yelling at her, telling her to mind her own goddamn business. After some minutes of squabbling, the next thing I saw was the two of them fighting and struggling over a butcher knife on the stairs. I couldn't believe what I was seeing. I slowly began to realize how big this problem really was, and that I was just a small part in the family's violence. Their violence was a way of life and he had grown up physically fighting with his mother!

I learned a lot about his mother and began to see that she was very different from my mother. She struggled to raise her five sons, some of them conceived by different fathers. All of the men had left her and she was desperate for money, even selling her body to get the money to feed them. She was strong, kind and caring, and her whole life could be seen in her sweet, sad eyes. Yet, there were still some undiscovered places in her which had been hardened by life. She was a real survivor, as are many other Black women.

I survived another horrible night, for that evening, we went to sleep with no words between us. In the middle of the night, I saw myself being gagged and tied up with cloth and a rope. As he tied my hands, he said, "I'm going to fix you. You embarrassed me in front of my mother and you're never going to do that again. I can kill you in a way that will look like an accident."

Then he opened the huge bay window in the bedroom, shoved me to the window and pushed half of my body over the window sill. We lived on the fourteenth floor and I knew if I fell out, I wouldn't survive. I screamed as loudly as I could, only to hear my own murmuring through the gag. My eyes widened and my crushing terror shifted into a smooth numbness. Resigned, I began to pray. After a moment, he hurriedly pulled me back in and quickly removed my restraints. He then immediately had sex with my body while I went someplace else.

Trapped!

When Doug and I went out on rare holiday occasions to visit relatives, I watched what I said—*if I said anything*—and acted appropriately. If I slipped up and said or did something that didn't meet his approval, he would furtively glare at me and quiver his left eye. That was a secret signal to expect violence when we got home.

At home, behind closed doors, when no one else was around to see him, he became Mr. Hyde.

Sometimes he would be violent and sometimes he wouldn't be. I was never really certain, and always stayed on edge, nervous, watchful and hyper-vigilant. His attacks, which were filled with accusations, were always surprise attacks. He was very crafty and skillful in the element of surprise and always caught me in a vulnerable state—in the bathtub, asleep, in my pajamas or washing my hair. He rarely got angry with me when I was actually cooking a meal or using a knife to chop vegetables.

I began to fear him and stopped looking into his eyes. I never seemed to be able to do anything he approved of. He was so nice to everyone else, sweet and charming in public, but at home, he became a demon—truly Dr. Jekyll and Mr. Hyde. I was sure no one would believe what I was going through with him. So, feeling isolated from friends, distant from my family, and minimized by his family, I felt hopeless, by myself and alone in this mess I'd created. Although I couldn't see a way out, I knew I had to find a way to cope until I could finally escape.

A year and a half passed while being with Doug, and I was still writing home and sending cards on occasion, assuring everyone that things were just fine. I was still angry with my father for a variety of reasons and not on speaking terms with him, and I rarely communicated with my family. I was, however, still close to my younger brothers and cared about how they were being treated by my Dad while still living at home. I knew it wasn't pleasant for them. In spite of my problems, I was driven to help them in whatever way I could. It was a good feeling to be able to send them money or to take out a loan for them. I really loved them and still do, very deeply.

I kept my deteriorating relationship to myself, away from my family. Only one close friend at work, my only friend, knew of my plight. Melinda was young, idealistic and Caucasian. She knew that something was wrong because whenever we talked, she kept asking me if I was doing okay. I worked hard to keep up my professional façade, denying that anything was wrong but she knew differently. She could tell by my strange reactions to certain topics and how I never talked about Doug. It took a lot of courage for me to finally tell her because I was a proud Black woman who did not want anyone's pity. I had really misjudged her.

When I did tell her, I told her everything—the Friday and Saturday night attacks, the frequent rapes, the lies, the drug use, and his unemployment. She immediately hated Doug and told me I deserved much better than him. She had a college degree in psychology and was able to direct me in some helpful ways. Sometimes I felt I was her test case but regardless, I was grateful for her kind and gentle help. Melinda was an angel friend for me, and because of her, I held on to a little bit of hope.

Several times, she and her husband rescued me from Doug, allowing me to stay at their apartment when he was on a rampage. I would call them on the phone and they would arrive to secretly take me away from there. They were wonderful, supportive friends and helped me erase my shame. She kept telling me to leave him, and I agreed that I needed to but couldn't see a safe way out at that time. More importantly, I couldn't envision a better life for myself without him. I wasn't ready.

Deep inside, I still believed Doug was the only one who could love me, that I was unworthy and that no one else would or could love me. I was sure I really couldn't do any better than Doug so I'd always go back to him after these episodes, believing it wouldn't happen again, while deep in my denial, I was determined to not provoke him in any way. I kept on believing his assertions that his violence was my fault.

I did my best to keep up appearances at work and try to pretend that everything was normal. I loved going to work and really felt appreciated and worthwhile at the office. I was a star performer and received performance awards and promotions. I was the model employee … so dedicated and such a workaholic! I even won a Young Career Woman Award. It was strange to receive an award like that while my personal life was a living hell. I felt like an imposter, thinking, "If they only knew …."

One Friday afternoon after work, I was sitting at the dinette table in my underwear with a loosely tied robe, daydreaming about a better life. I was even starting to think about ways to escape from him. A few moments later, he arrived with red eyes, drunk and high from some drug. I didn't speak to him and made the mistake of not preparing dinner. I saw the beating coming and ran out of the apartment and down the hallway yelling for help. My robe was flying open and I was in my underwear, pleading and screaming for help. He was angrily running after me.

A friendly, tall Caucasian woman let me into her apartment and I thanked her profusely. She told me to call the police, which I hesitated to do because I knew he would become even angrier after they left. Also I didn't want to get him in any more trouble with the law. I told her it wasn't that serious. She sternly looked at me and said, "Well, you're here in my apartment with a bathrobe on. Isn't that serious?"

We called the police and two officers arrived. They nonchalantly took a report and advised me to leave him because it would happen again. After this dialogue, I waited a while before going back to the apartment. I braced myself before entering, and was relieved to find out that Doug had disappeared.

The next day when he arrived home, he acted very, very sweet with flowers and a gift in hand. He asked me, "Why did you call the police?"

I replied, "The lady who helped me called them." I was working hard to defend myself by blaming it on her. He simply said, "They'll lock me up again."

I didn't say anything and stared blankly at the television. I was finally seeing his dysfunctional behavior pattern and in a defiant demonstration of my indifference to him, I didn't open the gift.

Over the next several months, I became more desensitized and detached from this skinny Black man I was living with. I watched him, hoping he would self-destruct. I repeatedly refused to join him in his hard drug use and I knew that, because of this, he sought out other female companions who would enjoy using with him. Really, he sought out other female companions anyway. I was no longer his beloved and had become his "meal ticket" and financial support system. The love between us had fallen off its fragile pedestal and lay shattered on the ground. There was no remedy for it; it was gone. Over.

Unfortunately, we were still having nonconsensual sex in which I was being raped regularly. Regardless of my pleas to not have sex, I felt I had no choice. I figured he had sex with me for two reasons. First, he didn't want me to think about having sex with another man when he wasn't around, and second, he wanted to ease his guilt about his sexual infidelities. The brutal perfunctory sex was painful, and I started to hate it. I thought about how he felt just like the guy in college who date-raped me. It felt like a strange, fleshy invasion. An unconnected object in me. Eventually, Doug's repeated invasions caused problems for me and I had to seek medical attention.

I slowly began to understand that Doug intended for me to have his child, which I think he believed would be the only way he could keep me imprisoned and attached to him forever. I also realized how he would have been a nightmare of a father. He'd already fathered a son by another woman, and six-year-old Kenny was already suffering from his abuse and neglect. I would spend time with him on the weekends while his father was out in the streets.

Teaching Doug's son was frustrating because whatever I taught him during the weekend was completely forgotten or abandoned the following weekend, after we'd returned him to his mother. We practiced reading a lot, I taught him good table manners and I helped him understand and appreciate animals. I also tried to teach him about how to treat people with respect and dignity, and I tried to protect and nurture him. Sometimes I felt I was wasting my time because nothing seemed to adhere. In spite of this uphill climb, I kept teaching him and eventually grew to love him. In fact, we became good pals.

Several years later, while driving to the Upper Marlboro Courthouse, I passed by the area where we'd lived and saw Kenny walking in the rain on the side of the highway. I wanted to stop and give him a ride, but couldn't because of the divorce agreement. Also, it would have sent the wrong message to his father. I really wished I could have saved him but learned later that he'd grown up to be just like his father.

Doug did not want me to use contraception. When I sensed rape was imminent, I would try to rush to the bathroom to insert my diaphragm but he would pre-empt my effort. He seemed to take a morbid delight in forcing me to have unprotected sex. He wanted me to have his child, but I told him our finances were too shaky and that it was not the right time. In truth, I had already realized he'd be a terrible father. Before each rape, I begged him not to do it, telling him I did *not* want to have any children. I also told him I'd get an abortion if he made me pregnant but it didn't make any difference. Using the elements of surprise and brute force, he kept raping me and I kept hoping to not conceive. I was repeatedly ravaged, physically and emotionally, and developed a sexual dysfunction. And, unfortunately, a few times, Doug succeeded and I did get pregnant.

Once I knew I was pregnant, I secretly got an abortion. I'd go to the clinic myself and take a taxi back home. After the third procedure at one clinic, a nurse told me I shouldn't be using abortion as contraception. I guess to her I looked like just another stupid Black girl. I told her I used a contraceptive whenever I could but she didn't understand the violent situation I was in. Nor did she seem to care. I was just another oversexed and ignorant Black girl to her.

One time, I went to the hospital to have a DNC, which is a euphemism for abortion. A few days later, while walking from the supermarket, I started to feel faint, very warm, and dizzy. My pants became very damp as I started to hemorrhage. When I arrived at the apartment, I immediately phoned the hospital and, after harsh and direct questioning, I hesitantly described my symptoms. The nurse told me to get to the hospital right away.

Once there, after a brief wait, I was told to remove my clothes. They guided me upon to the stirrups to give me a quick exam. Looking down at them, I searched their faces for an explanation. I watched the disgusted expression on the face of one of the nurses, who looked up at me and said, "The doctor who gave you the DNC didn't do a complete and thorough job." Because of his negligence, he'd left part of the fetus inside of me, and it had developed a major infection. The nurse added, "You could have died if you hadn't come in." The doctor gave me some antibiotics and told me to go home and rest. I took the subway home feeling very alone. Alone and trapped in my well-spun web of deception.

When I wasn't at work, I used television, alcohol and a regular weekend joint to obliterate my existence. I felt really stuck and completely incapable of sorting out the myriad emotions repressed within me. I just didn't want to feel the pain of this situation and anything that helped me temporarily numb out during the weekend was a very good thing.

Strangely, I attempted to take care of my health in other ways. I jogged regularly at a nearby park, worked out to Jane Fonda aerobic tapes, and played with a little Collie named Lucky, who lived near the park. When I jogged, I pretended I was running away from my problems. It felt great to escape temporarily from my reality. When I consistently worked out with a Jane Fonda tape, I listened to the song on the tape that said, "There's a calling inside you, driving you on ..." That tape helped me in a huge way and I slowly started to get a positive sense of myself, a glimmer of personal confidence and a little bit of hope for the possibility of a better life.

The Awakening

One Saturday morning, I arose in a very reflective yet guarded state. I mustered up the courage to quickly leave the apartment and treat myself to a new surrounding. I just walked and walked with no idea where I was going. I just felt like I needed to walk away from my problems that day. After about an hour, I came upon a little diner and figured I could stop in for a nice breakfast. It was a clean, casual place, and after glancing around the room, I was relieved to see no one who looked familiar. Feeling anonymous, I could relish the freedom to think my own very private thoughts.

While I sipped a really good cup of coffee, I reminisced on my grandmother's strength and how she dealt with lousy men, whereas I merely daydreamed about a new and better life. Inside, I struggled with my predicament. Something inside me seemed to be scratching at the surface, begging me to think of the beyond. It begged me to think of making one step outside and away from my predicament, from the horrible life I had created. I toyed with the idea of escaping, running away and wondering if I could really pull it off. I was worried about the idea of leaving because I thought of Doug as all-knowing. He seemed to know my thoughts, and was able to anticipate my every move. I felt that sure he would notice a change in my thoughts.

From all of the research I did when I was searching for a counseling service for Doug, I vaguely remembered the name of a counseling service that also had a hotline service for battered women, a 24-hour domestic abuse hotline somewhere in Bethesda, Maryland.

I called the number from a pay phone and was referred to a counselor. It felt so good to talk with someone who believed what I was going through, and who knew my pain and my struggle. Her voice had so much caring energy and hope in it that I talked for over two hours with the counselor, who encouraged me to come in to the center for counseling. After some deep thought and bolstered courage, I found a surreptitious way to get away to meet with her.

The counseling center had a modern, brightly painted and welcoming atmosphere. After completing some forms, I was directed to another room to talk with a counselor, a woman working on a doctoral study of abuse. She asked for my permission to use my interview in her thesis, which made me feel kind of special, so I agreed to let her use my personal information. She asked very probing questions and did not appear surprised by any of my answers.

I enjoyed talking about myself and my life. I loved being listened to and feeling affirmed. Then she asked, "How did you choose a man like this?" Suddenly I stumbled. I'd never thought about it and couldn't answer her.

She then asked me to describe my upbringing, my parents, home life, siblings and my choices. I shared my life story with her. As I talked, she listened, interjecting many exciting and sometimes difficult questions. I saw her for two counseling sessions.

During the second visit, she told me about the pattern of abuse and urged, "You need to leave your abuser and stay in a safe place with other women who have been abused. These men rarely stop the abuse. If they hit you once, they will hit you again and again. Many women overlook or minimize that first slap, but there's only a two percent chance that he could change and stop the violence."

In my mind, I saw myself in that "two percent" group, where the violent man changes his ways and becomes a healed, loving man. And of course, they both live happily ever after. The counselor told me about the helpful services provided to women, along with the superb police protection and progressive court system in the Montgomery County area.

I left that counseling session with a lot of information and was eager to learn more about domestic violence and why women stay in these bad situations. I was "intellectualizing" my plight, still unbelieving about how I was being abused and in personal, physical danger. I was still seeing myself as detached and removed from the drama of physical abuse. The deep love I once had for Doug and the growing dislike I was feeling towards his behavior seemed to confuse the dire facts of my situation. I was unaware of its depth.

The counselor had given me a two-page bibliography for domestic violence and I read every single book on the list. I obtained all of the facts and started to feel I knew what I was up against. I felt knowledge would be my power and that the more I knew, the more I'd be able to help Doug. I was determined to help him change because I believed in possibilities. Foolishly, I did not comprehend the magnitude of the situation.

I read horrible stories about women and domestic violence and felt sorry for the women who were ultimately killed by their boyfriends or spouses. At that time, I saw no possibility of me becoming one of them. I felt I was a part of a huge secret club of women in which race, class, education or profession didn't matter. Thousands of women were being beaten by their boyfriends or husbands who were Dr. Jekyll in public but, as soon as they were at home behind closed doors, they became Mr. Hyde. I got to know Mr. Hyde very well.

Despite the statistic that 98 percent of abusers never change, I still hoped Doug was one of the 2 percent who would make it. I had never failed at anything, and wanted so badly to succeed that I just couldn't let this relationship fail. I still didn't understand.

I still believed everything was within my control and that I was smart enough to dig my way out of this mess. I didn't want anyone's help. I wanted my friends and family to continue thinking how brainy and successful Gina was. My image was so important to me that I would even hide something like this from my family and friends. I wanted to destroy that voice in my head, echoing from years past, that kept saying, "You ain't gon' be shit." I had to prove I wasn't a failure, yet felt ashamed for being in such a plight. I beat myself up a lot, condemning my decisions, choices and actions. I felt like a loser, as if I was at the bottom of a deep well or in a canoe with a big leaky hole in it, or like a teenaged girl in a white dress with a big blood stain in the front of it. I was a little unattractive, insignificant Black girl with no audience.

I couldn't even talk to God about my situation because I had no relationship with Him or my spiritual self. I had lost my faith a long time ago so if I chose to go on, it would be just up to me. I knew I'd find a way to change my situation for the better because leaving Doug was not one of my options at that time. The counseling service was anonymous, so no one would ever know I went there for help, which I felt good about for I could keep up my professional, successful, fake image.

I was a romantic, believing in true love and possible change, so I was not ready to leave Doug. I felt that if only I could understand my situation a little better, I'd be able to help him change. I knew he loved me a lot and that we could make it as a young Black couple. I didn't want to give up on him and believed he would see how his behavior affected me. Naively, I was totally unaware of how deep his violent world was.

Back to Normal

*A*fter all of the reading about domestic violence, I became better
able to see the world around me and observed many things
with a new lens. While I worked hard to become more perfect at
home to stave off his violence, I became a silent observer of his
social world. I noticed how the women in his family, his in-laws and
those who had relationships with his brothers were unassertive,
subservient and silent. I noticed how they did not stand up for their
own needs, wants or desires. Whenever we engaged in conversations
about "our men" and their behaviors, a slow and gradual nonverbal
resignation filled the room. Of course, there were all the excuses,
justifications and denials about the poor reality of the situation, and
I knew I would not find an ally to help me challenge or try to change
the way things were.

I felt Doug's constant pressure on me to become like them. He
seemed to hold in high esteem the fact that they didn't complain
about anything, overlooked infidelities, frequent unemployment and
regular hard drinking, and took on the burdens of all the work in and
outside the home. And finally, they overlooked their yearning for a
better life for *themselves*.

My different thinking began to alienate me from them. I did my
best to be nice and sociable, but deep inside, I felt there might be
other choices for me. Meanwhile, Doug seemed to be content but
watched me closely for any assertive behavior changes.

With increasingly regular surprise attacks, I became more com-
pliant and fearful of him. Just when I would start to believe things
were getting better because of a lull in the violence, there would be
another attack. Trying to exert some control over my life, I sought to
predict his violent episodes. I noted strategic spots to place a knife or
a heavy object, but it would never work out the way I'd planned. He
had the uncanny ability to always find me unaware, vulnerable and
half-dressed.

My hyper-vigilance and anxiety heightened as I tried to guard
myself against his attacks 24/7. I learned to watch his eyes closely

and listen for certain key words he would use. Whenever he looked at me and flinched his right eye, I knew I would be in trouble once we were home and behind closed doors. I felt running away wouldn't solve anything because when he found me, the beating would be twice as bad. He was an enemy I was destined to share my life with. He was pure evil.

I continued to endure him and the violence, learning to know myself as ugly, stupid, and lazy. I was invisible at home and in the mirror. Everyday, I was bombarded with a string of negative descriptions of me—stupid, ugly and lazy were his favorites. No more "sweetness," as he once used to call me.

Doug became really angry if I didn't have any money to give him for alcohol or drugs. After a particularly horrific violent episode one Friday night, before leaving on the following Saturday morning, he placed the usual joint for me on the coffee table. I quickly packed it in my bag because I had finally resolved to leave him. Earlier, I had lied about needing the car for some badly needed grocery shopping and drove my BMW to the counseling center. As I drove with a mixture of resolve and mild terror, I lit up the joint and inhaled quickly, just to get through the uncertainty ahead.

Three Weeks in a Shelter for Battered Women

At the counseling center, I found myself in a brightly painted and organized office area. I mumbled my way through the intake process, feeling lost and ashamed, and avoided eye contact with anyone. I discovered that hidden in the back of the building and upstairs were a kitchen, dorm rooms, bathrooms and a sitting area. It was a well-disguised shelter for battered and abused women, and the first rule I learned was to never let anyone know where the shelter was located.

My shame subsided for a while as I looked at the 15 other women staying there. They were all of different races, classes and religions.

I felt so sorry for them and cried during our group sessions when I heard of some of their stories. One tall brown-skinned lady, who reminded me of my Aunt Dorothy, had been kicked repeatedly in the stomach by her husband while he was wearing his steel-toed construction boots.

One lady told me of her frequent trips to the hospital for surgery due to her man's violence. Another talked about being violated repeatedly with object rape. The stories I heard made my episodes seem rather mild and insignificant, and I started to think my situation wasn't so bad because I never had to go to the hospital for broken ribs or a broken jaw.

Feeling more fortunate than the others, after a few days, I began to long for Doug. Without him, I felt empty and incomplete, and it seemed as if I couldn't breathe without him around. He was my "other half," a plight I would come to call "codependence." I always thought that meant one person was truly in love with another. Many love songs talk about the "longing and emptiness inside"; and there are many of these popular "codependent" songs on the radio and television, describing how "I can't live without you."

I enjoyed my days at the shelter because I could put my worry aside and felt part of a big loving family. Of course, we all had chores to do and lots of counseling sessions. However, all of those probing questions during the sessions made me feel uncomfortable. I really didn't think my situation was *that* bad, and the persistence of the counselors that there was a serious problem got on my nerves.

I began to like the comradeship and the new information I was learning about domestic violence. We could stay at the shelter for up to three weeks, during which we were forbidden any contact with the abuser. At the end of her stay, each woman was directed to find a new place to live, for the domestic abuse cycle was broken only with complete separation from the abuser. This all had to occur in complete secrecy because batterers are crafty and charming, and often find ingenious ways to recapture their prey.

At the shelter, a movie was shown every Friday night, and we would all sit around in the living room in our pajamas, making hot buttery popcorn and acting like chatty little girls, all of us feeling very safe during these gatherings. One Friday night we watched the movie *The Burning Bed* starring Farrah Fawcett, on a major television network. It was cutting-edge television, and a real breakthrough!

We all watched the television, enthralled and mesmerized, thinking our story could be on television, too. At certain points, someone would verbally sympathize with the victim. I couldn't get over the fact that there I was in a domestic violence shelter watching a movie about domestic violence. Life does imitate art! I began to realize that my life was like a soap opera—so much drama! I didn't need to watch the soaps; my life *was* a soap opera.

It wasn't all about fun and group support at the shelter, however. I befriended one of the women who later thought I'd told her boyfriend where she went to live, because he found her and violently attacked her once again. It hurt me to think she could believe I had betrayed her like that. So, in other ways, it was a horrible, dark time there, and my heart ached for her.

I refrained from smoking pot on the weekends because it wasn't allowed at the shelter. I spent my time near the book shelves, reading the fascinating stories about domestic violence, with many of the stories being much, much worse than mine.

I began to go through the motions of finding a new place to live, and pondered what it would be like to live alone, without Doug unsure if I would enjoy it. I found a new apartment, but it was in the same apartment building as the place I'd shared with Doug. Thank goodness I was able to transfer my current lease to this new apartment, since I'd been paying the rent on time. I guess I subconsciously didn't want to be too far away from him.

With each passing day, I began to feel stronger and more capable of leaving him, especially since I found out it was okay to call the police if he ever approached me. In Montgomery County, the police responded very quickly to domestic violence calls. The county was very progressive and innovative in dealing systemically with domestic violence, with the police, courts and judges all sending the same strong message of low tolerance toward abusers. This was a blessing for me. I was also told I could file for a restraining order against him, if he disregarded my directives to stay away. If he violated the restraining order, he would be sent to jail.

Because of his past record, I didn't want to file a restraining order against him, thinking he would have to go back to jail. I still cared for him deeply and wanted to protect him. I still believed that he deserved to be treated well. I was still programmed to think that men always came first.

My Apartment

I eventually settled into a newly painted, one-bedroom, sterile apartment. I remember sitting in the kitchen, looking blankly around at the walls, wondering how I was going to exist like this, all alone. I managed to move my body through each day, with a hard longing for Doug's male company. I felt hopeless because I just knew that no one else was going to love me like he did. I liked how he smothered me and consumed every moment of my life. I craved his attention because it seemed to fill a void from my past. I enjoyed being devoted to him, and it was difficult to see a future without him. I minimized my thoughts of the violence, dismissing them and seeing the violence as just regular arguments between loving mates.

In spite of these torn feelings, I obeyed the counselors and didn't contact him or his family. I was totally isolated with no friends nearby. Since Doug had found creative ways to control my social life, I found myself with few if any friends. Most of them had disappeared due to my inattentiveness towards them, but it was mostly due to Doug's strong criticism of them that had encouraged me to drop them.

After about two weeks in the new apartment, I had adjusted to my new routine of going to work each day and to the grocery store when I needed to stock up on some basics. I really didn't cook much for myself because I had not learned how to honor myself with a great meal. I could cook a great meal for someone else but not for myself.

Then, one morning, while I was walking to my car in the dark basement garage, Doug suddenly jumped up out of nowhere and surprised me. He put a hand over my mouth and whispered in my ear, "Don't scream. I have a gun." I shut up immediately, and began to sob through his hand, making muffled my pleas for him to go away and leave me alone. My eyes tried to express everything that I felt—anguish, pity, sorrow, disgust, and hopelessness. He forced me into my car, took the keys from me, and began driving. While he drove, he kept saying, "If I can't have you, nobody will."

I sat quietly, wishing I could disappear and float away. When the car stopped, he made me get out and walked me through the entrance of a rundown apartment building in the southeast part of the city. He directed me to sit still, to not scream and told me I was going to stay there with him all day. He tied me up and stripped me naked. At some point, much later that night, he told me to get dressed and then drove me back home.

He told me not to tell anyone or else they would lock him up again. He whispered how much he missed me and loved me and tears rolled down his face as he claimed how he would never hit me again. He begged me to let him come back and live with me. I didn't say anything to this mentally ill and helpless man. Instead, I felt sorry for him yet at the same time, I knew I had to file for a restraining order to keep him away from me. I resolved to not mention the kidnapping to the police.

The next day, feeling exhausted and in a haze, I went to work debating with myself about whether I should file for a restraining order. I told my only friend at work what had happened, and she told me to go to the police. I didn't want the police involved, yet I knew it would be the only way to stop the abuse.

After work, I slowly walked towards the police station, repeating the mantra of the counselors: "The only way to change his behavior is to tell the police." I definitely wanted his behavior to change, but felt this was an extreme way to do it. I just wanted him to just stop. Why couldn't he just stop? Once at the local police station, after a 45-minute wait in the reception area, I was directed to an officer at a desk. She was a stern-looking Black woman and began the questioning. I was hesitant, feeling ashamed and stupid when she asked me why I wanted to file for the restraining order. I told her, "My ex-boyfriend is trying to get back in touch with me and would hurt me again if I don't file."

She nonchalantly completed the form and requested my signature. She told me, "If he violates the restraining order, he'll be sent to jail."

I left the station feeling different—a little safer but also as though I'd just betrayed Doug. I was still wandering from day to day, feeling mildly incomplete without him. I had no conviction about anything other than that my life was in chaos and that I was unhappy. I even began to harbor a mild regret for going to the women's shelter and starting all these changes in my life.

One month after I'd moved into my new apartment, I gathered my purse and briefcase to leave for work. As I turned the key in the door to lock it, Doug was suddenly standing there, right next to me. I calmly told him, "I've filed a restraining order and you need to leave." Ignoring that, he forced me to reopen the door and go back inside. I told him, "I'm going to be late for work."

He didn't seem to care and asked, "What do you have in the refrigerator to eat?"

I told him, "You can check the refrigerator, because I have to go to the bathroom." Although I did have to go to the bathroom, I also called the police from my bedroom, as directed by the women's shelter. When I returned to the kitchen, I wondered how long it would take for the police to arrive, while I strived to stay calm and indifferent.

Doug didn't have a car anymore and he asked if I could drop him off someplace on my way to work. I knew this was a trick of his to get back into the car and to take control of the situation. I told him, "No. because I'm already late for work." Minutes passed and I was still stalling for time in anticipation that the police would arrive to take him away. I convinced him to let me leave for work and, as we left my apartment, he walked with me towards the garage. As we approached the lobby, I looked up and saw a police officer. Doug suddenly took off running.

I began to feel some relief at the sight of the officer, but not much because I noticed that the officer was rotund. I identified myself to him and pointed in the direction I'd seen Doug running. I began running along with the officer to show him the layout of the apartment complex so that he might catch Doug. We went up some stairs and down others, through a side alley and through the garage. It was quite a workout but as a jogger, I easily outpaced him. The officer had to slow down to catch his breath so I doubled back to talk with him. After a moment of his hard breathing, we went back to my apartment to complete the police report.

When the officer left, I called my office to let my boss know I'd be late. Cautiously I went to my car and began driving to work, feeling a little angry at the fat policeman for not being able to catch Doug. But my anger melted when I realized what I had courageously done. I had called the police to report Doug, which was an important first step for me. It was something new for me, yet I felt awkward about it.

Not Yet Healed

Days and weeks passed, but no day ever passed without my thinking of Doug, how things could have been different between us, and about whether he could change miraculously. Also about whether he had found someone new to spend time with. I compared our violence to my parents' fighting when I was younger and wondered whether it was just a routine part of a loving relationship, like communication. I started to believe that maybe I could have done things differently, that maybe I had not tried hard enough to understand him and love him. I believed that love conquered everything, and thought that maybe I hadn't loved him enough. He'd had such a rough life, and with my love, he could blossom and grow into a powerful, capable and loving man. I thought of Doug often. Too often.

The subconscious mind is a very powerful vehicle. I say this because I really wondered whether I subconsciously desired to reconnect with Doug. I had really convinced myself I needed him in my life. Meanwhile, I went about my dreary life, feeling unloved and alone, dutifully working towards my imagined career goals. I went to work each day, exceeding the tasks and objectives that were required of me because my job was my only reason for living. I loved my job and was able to forget about my miserable personal life while I was at work.

I spent my time helping others, working to improve the workplace for blue collar employees. I loved working with the Quality Circles Program at the Department of Navy. I could see the positive results of my efforts in the smiles of the employees whenever they enjoyed a repainted lunch room, a larger parking area or any other workplace improvement. Any small achievement at work gave me great pleasure and made me feel I was worth something. My job was my fulfillment.

I desperately wanted to feel in control of something and my job gave me that satisfaction. I had no ideas or beliefs about letting God be in control of my life because my faith was practically non-existent at that time. Although I prayed on occasion, it was empty and distant. Deep down inside, I still believed my life quality was up to me. Any mistakes I made were my fault, my stupidity. I would do my best to not make any mistakes, and believed that only I could repair my mistakes when necessary.

One Saturday evening, I was returning from an exhausting day of afternoon errands and stopped at a familiar gas station to fill up the tank. Just as I was getting back into my BMW, I heard someone calling my name. I looked up and saw Doug approaching me. I hurriedly locked the door, fastened my seat belt and started the ignition. He softly moved his face up to the window and I immediately saw the desperation and sadness in his eyes, something I'd never seen before.

His eyes pleaded with me and begged me for just one moment of my time. I looked away, hung my head down and then quickly glanced back at him, locking my eyes with his. I stared at him, feeling pity and compassion for him, yet I was still afraid of him. I longed for him, for he had been my soul mate and my savior but also my demon. I felt that the story of us, our beautiful, romantic story with the happy ending, had not yet ended.

I got out of the car and hugged him. He started to cry and began apologizing for his past actions. He sobbed that he wanted us to be together and that he would never, ever hurt me again. He told me how much he loved me and couldn't live without me. He said everything I wanted to hear and even got down on his knees and begged me to give him another chance. I melted and decided to give him a second chance. I convinced myself that every human being deserves a second chance. I realized we all make mistakes and that we all should be forgiven, no matter how horrid the mistakes were. So I forgave him. I really loved him, needed him and believed we could start anew. I knew he would live up to the man I believed him to be. I would risk it all again to try again.

Back in Love Again

Without hesitation, I gave Doug my new phone number. During our first long conversation, he made me promise to remove the restraining order at the courts. After I did this, we eagerly began making plans together about saving to buy a house. He told me he had not been with anyone else, that he just wanted to get back together with me. I was elated to hear this and realized we were truly meant for each other.

We decided to move out of my apartment and rent something else, which would allow us to save more money. We moved into an older apartment in Bladensburg, Maryland. The rent was a lot less and there were flying roaches, but the porch was nice. I felt like I was regressing because, to me, the apartment felt like an old housing project—run down, poorly maintained lawns, and uneducated neighbors. I really liked the porch though and spent many days and nights with my Hibatchi stove, Bacardi coolers and a joint, which helped me believe everything would be just great (or at least not so bad).

I saved money furiously and Doug worked intermittently, adding to the savings when he could. The first few months were pleasant and warm. Doug bought me flowers and gifts frequently. Our love-making was at first fantastic, but then it became detached and routine. Although there were no episodes of violence, Doug seemed to be absent a lot. And, when we did spend time together, we were often collecting money from strange acquaintances, entertaining assorted visitors or just chatting idly with female guests who his brothers dated. I was learning to not ask questions, so I just silently observed and wondered how they all met each other, so often and so quickly.

One time during the holidays, Doug disappeared for several days. I stayed at home, calling around, crying and wondering whether something had happened to him. When he returned, he was cavalier and indifferent, providing a cryptic answer about working on a project when I asked him where he'd been. I believed him and slowly began to accept things as they were. In my denial, I stopped searching for real answers and learned to accept the canned lies I was often fed. Often, I'd just sit in the living room, looking out the windows, watching the birds and enjoying the clouds. I'd spend hours standing or just sitting at the window.

As the weeks and months passed, I regressed into a passive, unaware and undeclared woman. I had finally learned "my place" and had decided I would be a nice, quiet, obedient woman who was loved by a misunderstood and complex Black man. I was determined to see our co-dependent relationship as all right. Our relationship was not perfect, but it wasn't bad either, because he had refrained from hitting me and was not sleeping with other women. I still had hope. I had a *lot* of anticipation as I daydreamed about someday having our nice, warm home together. I longed for a cozy home with a husband, for someone to wake up to, someone to cook for and someone to achieve dreams with me. I wanted to complete my fantasy picture of happiness.

Our New Home

*M*onths passed and money was saved. When we reached over $5,000, we knew that a home would be possible as first-time buyers and began searching. Our real estate agent was a Black woman who was amicable and understanding but not very efficient. We were pestered with sending and faxing numerous individual documents for several weeks, without a comprehensive explanation.

We spent Saturdays looking at different homes in the areas of Camp Springs, Suitland, Bladensburg and Silver Spring, Maryland. We finally found a cute, 2-bedroom home in Suitland with a mother-in-law suite downstairs. It had a red and brick exterior with a fireplace and garage, a crepe myrtle tree out front and a huge back yard. I would finally be able to get a dog and have lots of pets!

Finally, owning a home would be one more goal I would achieve on my road to success! I was driven to achieve the American dream and knew that Doug would change for the better, once we began living together in a home that we'd bought together. I remember telling him, "I don't want to just live together anymore. If we buy a home together, we should be married." Even though I knew I'd be paying the mortgage along with most of the bills, the thought of being on my own and leaving Doug was too dangerous.

The only alternative left was to legitimize the relationship by getting married. Doug agreed, although reluctantly, and when the subject of a ring came up, I told him not to because we could put the money towards the new home. I thought a ring would be a waste of money at that time.

We got married on Valentine's Day, February 14, 1987, which was also my mother's birthday. We went to the Justice of the Peace and had it done with no fanfare. I didn't even call home to tell my Dad because we were still in the middle of a non-speaking "cold war" at the time, which lasted several years. I was still angry with him over many family issues and how he had treated me.

Once married, I did not change my last name, which angered Doug. He felt it showed I didn't love him enough. I told him, "It's important for me to keep my own name. It's all I have." I stood firm on this issue and even surprised myself with my own conviction. I may have been a doormat and a little mouse at the time, but there were a few things I adhered to.

We moved into our new home in June 1987. We were jubilant! It was picture perfect! Once married, I thought of the lasting state of matrimony and remembered the words: "Til death do us part." I thought of how happy I was supposed to be. "I'm married! This is it! This is my new life!"

However, as the days progressed, I became more aware of how things were not picture perfect. Doug reverted back to his old ways, only with more fervor. I began to strategize around his crazy behavior to protect myself. I became even more hyper-vigilant and anxious when he was near. When alone, I felt resigned, numb and insensitive to my surroundings. My soul got up and left. My spirit died. There was nothing left to keep me intact except my pets. I had a bunny, some turtles and two dogs.

Animal Grace

Several months passed while I dwelled on the fact that my long awaited picture of happiness and bliss was not being realized. Being married, I had no way out of this situation. Doug began to revert back to his old habits of staying out all night, dealing drugs and beating me. The only bright spot in the marriage was his professed fidelity towards me. He had mentioned repeatedly that he was loyal to me and would never cheat on me. This made me feel better because I realized he really did love me and was just a sick man who needed me.

Daunted about my situation, I focused on the happiness my job and my pets gave me. My pets kept me living each day, and, when things got really bad and I contemplated suicide, I never went through with it because I loved my animals. If I committed suicide, they would be left on their own with no one to care for them. It was a good thing they were in my life and gave me so much joy. I wanted to stay in the happy world of my beloved turtles, bunny, and dogs. We even traded in the BMW for a Chevy Blazer so the dogs would have more space.

My pets helped keep me alive, but I also thought of the selfishness involved in the act of suicide. I wondered how people could think only of themselves. What about their family and the friends they leave behind? I just couldn't do that to my Dad and my brothers and sisters. Just the thought of them wondering how they might have intervened would have been heart-wrenching. No, suicide was not an option for me.

I found solace with my two dogs, a Doberman named Star and a German Shepherd named Silvie. They jogged with me on the weekends and were very good, loyal dogs who protected me whenever they felt I was in danger. Silvie would growl at Doug whenever he approached me or yelled at me. Eventually, Doug became crafty and began to put the dogs outside in the backyard before unleashing his cruelties.

What pushed me near the edge was the unpredictability of his violence. If I expected his violence every day, it never happened. Then, when I thought things were getting better, he'd rail up against me again with physical abuse. I began to hide the kitchen knives and any other objects I thought he could use to harm me. I also learned to hide money so that I would at least have bus fare when he took the car. Each waking moment was about planning and anticipating the worst from him. I could never relax, for when I did, it was always with a beer or the occasional joint. Feeling "alive and in the moment" was painful, and I postponed it as long as I could with alcohol.

To Doug, I was worthless and could never do anything right. Dinner was either too cold, or not enough or the wrong kind. I was either too lazy to clean the house, or getting on his nerves from cleaning too much. I was getting more stupid and more ugly and fake. I was getting "too big for my britches" and flirting with his friends. The more success I achieved at work, the more he criticized me. Although I received awards and acknowledgements at work, no one there knew of my private hell at home. Thank God for my job, where I could be that "great professional woman."

I loved my work and worked hard to earn money. Unfortunately, a lot of it went to Doug, who would become instantly furious if I didn't have any money to give him. Our money seemed to disappear like rain on a hot sidewalk. I dreaded going to the mailbox due to all the letters from the bill collectors. I did everything I could to keep current with the bills, but to no avail. One too many times, I believed him whenever he would promise he would have money on a certain day to pay a bill that was overdue, but it was always a lie. I was not familiar with the constant, creative lying by a drug user. By the time I did stop believing in his promises about another new job or some money owed to him, we were close to having very bad credit.

Doug's "business" seemed to thrive around the holidays because he was never at home during those times. When he knew he would be away for a long time, he would "medicate" me with a joint, saying, "I'll be right back." Those words usually meant I'd see him at four in the morning or the next day. I was used to this drill and I accepted the pain-free token. At least when he wasn't home, I had the certainty of my own stillness.

On the weekends, when I had the time and courage to think, I tried to drown my pain with wine and beer. It hurt when I thought about my life and my dashed dreams, so I decided to start doing volunteer work to prevent me from thinking about my life. It did. I did a lot of volunteer work as my escape. It kept my mind off of me and my dismal life, for the more I thought of others, the less time I had to focus on my sad life.

Look Ma, a Busted Lip!

I was way beyond just feeling sad. I had created this mess I was in, and I was stuck deeply in it. Miss "Successful Career Woman" was not so successful. What a sham! Going to work each day as if my life were normal. I wanted to talk to someone I could trust, and often longed for my Mom, despite some residual, internal anger towards her for dying and leaving us. I started to hope that perhaps Doug's mother would like me and maybe even be my replacement Mom. She even looked like my real mom.

One Easter Sunday, after Doug had just punched me in the face the night before, his mother came to visit us. I thought the timing of her visit was great. I felt hopeful because I finally had something to prove the violence inflicted by her son—a busted, swollen lip! This was real evidence she would see and perhaps she would finally believe me about the "problems" we were having.

When she saw my busted, swollen lip, she ignored it, her conversation continuing in its amicable tone. I was in disbelief about her indifference and touched my lip to make sure it was still there, swollen. It was, and even felt even bigger. I really wanted more out of this moment, for her to really see me, to acknowledge my agony. So, I boldly stated, "Your son punched me in the face last night." She looked blankly at me and pulled out her Bible to read some passages to me. I was dumbstruck by her reaction and quickly realized I would never get a hug of compassion from her with her son standing there. I even thought for a brief moment that she was afraid of him.

A few weeks later, this was proved true. We were at her house one evening and I began to talk about her son's behavior. She listened intently and told me, "Work with him. He needs understanding from a good woman like you."

I was hurt and disappointed because she seemed more concerned about someone keeping her violent son content than my concerns about being safe and protected. I sat in the living room waiting for Doug, slowly absorbing this bleak and disappointing information from his mother. From the window, I saw him quickly drive up and park in the front of the house. In a tempestuous mood, he flung the front door open and walked straight back to the kitchen where his mother was washing dishes and storing leftovers from dinner.

From the kitchen, voices become louder, more vicious, with crude profanity used. I looked towards the kitchen and saw Doug's mother with a knife in one hand, pushing him away with the other. They fought their way upstairs, both of them clutching the huge kitchen knife. I couldn't believe my eyes. I was immobilized in the living room chair, watching this extreme act of potentially deadly violence play out for the second time.

It seemed to last for hours, but it was only for a minute. The fight ended as quickly as it started. I had no idea how the fight started or what had caused the words to escalate into violence. The tension quelled and I was relieved to get out of that house, but I was also very anxious about what was in store for me when we arrived home. I felt he would probably blame me for rousing his mother. That night he surely did.

Stopping the Violence

Somehow, once again, I got the courage to call the police when Doug became violent. I soon stopped looking into his eyes and just anticipated the first surprise blow out of nowhere. Often, the attacks were in the middle of the night when I was half asleep and wearing little clothing. I called the Prince George County police often.

Occasionally, Doug's little son, Kenny, would be there to observe the violence. I felt bad that he had to see such poor adult behavior. Kenny was gentle and sweet, and would spend some weekends with me. I continued to teach him new activities, such as cooking and caring for pets, and enjoyed his curiosity, patiently answering all his many questions. He made me laugh a lot, too, and we developed a strong bond against his abusive father. He was our common enemy.

I got educated about how to work with the police and follow the routine for filing complaints. However, I lost some faith in the police when, on one violent occasion, a Black police officer made a pass at me while I was in my underwear, vulnerable and crying. He seemed to be more focused on my body than on my dangerous situation. It all seemed so absurd. If I couldn't trust a police officer, who in the world could I trust?

Gone All the Time

Well, I finally had my dream house in a big dream that went sour. Many nights I'd lie in bed wondering where my husband was. I had very little feeling left in my being and tears would no longer come. I had finally recognized and relented to the fact that I had married a monster.

To cope with this failure, I pushed those thoughts out of my head and focused on my job and the exciting volunteer work I was doing. The image I tried to maintain was one of helping and giving to others, which was what I really wanted and needed—attention, time, and caring. I managed the household finances as much as possible, trying to maintain good credit, in spite of the odds from living with a lying, cheating cocaine and heroin addict.

I volunteered a lot and worked long hours at my job a lot—anything to keep my mind off the thoughts of home. To get better at managing the household finances, I enrolled in an income tax class, which was fun and well-structured. I was doing quite well in the class, religiously doing my homework at the dining room table on Friday nights.

The Phone Call

On the evening of Friday, November 20, 1987, the phone rang. It was a woman who asked, "Is this Gina?" I answered yes and she went on to say, "My name is Lia. I found out that you and Doug just got married. Did you know that on the night before you got married, he was with me? We bought a horse together and now I'm in debt over this horse. We went to West Virginia together, his clothes are over here and he has keys to my apartment. He told me he doesn't have sex with you anymore, and wants me to have his baby. I know a lot of secrets about you because he tells me everything about you."

As she was speaking, my hand was shaking as I tried to take notes from her call. I was taking notes! Taking those notes probably kept me from losing my mind. Everything seemed to be moving in slow motion, as I absorbed what she was saying. I could hear Doug's voice in the background while she was speaking telling her to hang up the phone. Hearing his voice coming from her phone pierced my heart. The last thing she said before hanging up was that she had been in a relationship with Doug for the last year and a half.

I hung up the phone, devastated and frozen in place for a while. Then, strangely, I went back to doing my homework. When I finished, I got up from the table and my mind started doing funny things, like weaving in and out of the fragmented realities. I was picturing all kinds of situations my husband had created, which were now being erased. I went to the kitchen and drank everything that contained alcohol.

Hours passed. Still wanting to change the truth I had just heard, I decided to ask Doug about it when he returned. Maybe I'd get another version. I was thinking that he could have another chance to deny it. When he came home that morning, he was more confident than ever. We said nothing to each other until the phone rang. It was Lia again. That Saturday afternoon, at 1:00pm, Lia and I both confronted Doug in a 3-way telephone conversation. It's almost as if Lia and I shared a common enemy. We both hated him. Doug said he wouldn't stop seeing Lia because he feels the same way for both of us. When I heard that, I realized everything was over. I was not an adored wife. I was being used just to keep a roof over his head and provide a decent car for him to drive around in.

Everything was broken and wrong. Betrayed, beaten and used, I was nothing. Later that day, I overheard Doug on the telephone in the bedroom telling Lia that he could get our marriage annulled. At that moment, I felt a searing pain shoot through my gut. Here was my husband discussing with the "other woman" how he was going to dispose of me.

From that day, he kept calling her on the phone, acting as if I wasn't there anymore. When he did talk to me, he was brazen and bold, acting as if he was finally glad the truth was out. He became more defiant and even meaner, and looked at me one day and said, "What you gonna do about it, bitch?"

That holiday season was the bleakest ever. I managed to get through Thanksgiving and Christmas alone, with Doug spending most of this time with Lia. I was spending my time putting the pieces together from the past, now understanding better some of those things that were never fully explained to me at the time. For example, his disappearance for several days, the red nail polish on the new sweater I had bought him, the 4 a.m. arrivals, the regular telephone "hang-ups," the perfunctory sex, his happiness when I had to go away on travel, the unanswered telephone calls, and all the lies.

I began to think about harming him. I thought about hitting him really hard on the head with one of the fireplace pokers. Then I thought about the consequences. I did not want to go to jail for the rest of my life, for *my* life would be ruined and *he* would win. I realized something had to change, but I didn't know what or how. I was afraid of him, and part of me knew he was going to kill me eventually.

The Soul in the Mirror

A few weeks later, on a Saturday afternoon in January, I went into the bathroom with the intention of cutting all my hair off. I wanted to change something about myself, so I began cutting my hair, taking chunks of it, chopping it off and watching it fall into the sink. I looked up into the bathroom mirror and slowly put the scissors down. I looked deeply into my own eyes for a long time and I saw something different. As I stared into me, I heard a still small voice say, "This is not how your life is supposed to be. You deserve to be happy. You deserve so much more. You can leave him."

I began to cry and then cried some more. When my crying stopped, a calmness and conviction enveloped me. I started to plan.

Over the next several days, I began to think about how I could leave him. I knew I would be facing danger because he had repeatedly told me he would "set me up" or plant drugs on me if I had tried to leave him. He had also mentioned quite frequently that if he couldn't have me, no one else would, either. He had threatened to kill me on many occasions and I believed he would.

I began thinking about a plan. Since I did all of the household finances, the taxes and the bills, I could surely think of something. I decided to wait until February to leave, as I could take the tax refund check and pay an attorney for a divorce. In the meantime, I continued life as usual so that Doug wouldn't suspect what I was planning.

In late February of 1988, I got a referral from an acquaintance for a divorce attorney. Luckily, I got the Blazer on a weekday and drove to his office. I explained my situation to the attorney, whose rate was $200 an hour, and gave him the meager deposit of $2,500. For the first time, with courage, I explained the abuse, the betrayal and the violence to this stranger. He listened intently as he shook his head in disgust. He explained to me that I would need some good evidence of the marital infidelities, records describing the abuse, or anything else that would bolster my case. I thanked him and left. He and his paralegal started to complete the paperwork. I went back to the house, thinking of my next steps. I knew I would have to leave suddenly, without many clothes or even my pets. I just didn't know when. When would be the best time to do it?

The following week, I polled the neighborhood of surrounding homes, interviewing the home owners, trying to obtain a witness for one of our past domestic violence incidents. I specifically asked each one whether they had heard any of my screaming during the previous weeks, but no one, not one person, had heard anything. At the end of all this, if they hadn't known of the physical abuse I was enduring, they all knew after my house-to-house polling! It was very humiliating and embarrassing to ask each one of the neighbors about the fights and screaming, yet I was so intent on gaining some credible evidence that I swallowed my pride and worked hard to find witnesses.

I hired a detective service to try to obtain pictures of him as he was leaving his girlfriend's house. Executing this strategy gave me a strange and positive sense of having some control over something in my life. It was empowering! Unfortunately, after spending $700, they weren't able to take any pictures. My attorney told me to save my money and forget about the detective service.

Final Escape: A Walk by Faith

One evening Doug's son, Kenny, and I were doing some homework at the dining room table. I was doing my income tax homework and Kenny was doing his school homework. Suddenly, we heard the keys jingle at the door, and Doug appeared. He was visibly upset and full of tension. We sensed that something dreadful was about to happen. We were both accustomed to that weird feeling in the air and both knew Doug was about to go into a rage. Sure enough, he did. Like all the other times, we had no idea what caused his rage. Maybe it was because I didn't prepare a special dinner for him. Maybe it was because Kenny was not dressed for bed yet. Maybe it was because we both appeared content without him. Maybe there was no reason.

Doug began yelling at us, using his fists on both me and Kenny to emphasize his points. I ran to the bedroom to call the police. Kenny escaped and also ran to the bedroom while we both waited for the police to arrive, hoping that Doug would soon calm down. The officers arrived in about 10 minutes, since they were already quite familiar with our residence. I explained the violent situation and told them I wanted to press charges this time. It was as if another person was speaking the words "press charges." I had never done that before, because usually when the officers came to the house, I'd listen to Doug's pleading and have mercy on him, so wouldn't press assault charges. This time it was really different and I followed through on the promise to myself.

Doug couldn't believe his ears when he heard me say that. He gave me that horrible look with his eyes that said, "I'm going to kill you when I get the first chance." We watched as the officers handcuffed Doug and led him away to the police car. One officer remained behind and told me, "You'd better get some things together and leave the house immediately. You don't want to be here when he returns."

I knew I had to leave because I knew he was going to come back, searching for me to kill me. I walked away from the house that day, a house that was a hard-earned venture and a precious piece of my romantic fantasy of living "happily ever after." Although I walked away from that house, I began to walk through my fear that day. It felt as if I was walking out onto thin air, with nothing under my feet. I was leaving Doug behind me, and in front of me was the unknown. A chasm of separation and uncertainty. It was my first step out on faith. Faith in the miraculous possibilities by God. Faith that He would protect me. All I had was that awkwardly awakened faith. I let go of the past and surrendered my fear to a Higher Power. It happened in a moment. One warm, golden moment.

Kenny and I walked quickly to the car, small bags of hastily packed clothing under our arms. I ran to collect the dogs, my real friends. I wanted them with me because I knew I would not be returning, so I loaded them quickly into the back of the Blazer. I drove by Kenny's house, stopped there to greet his mother and explain I was leaving Doug. Kenny and I hugged goodbye for a long time and I told him to be good and to do his homework. I felt I would never see him ever again.

I impulsively decided to go to the home of the friend who had given me the legal reference, a warm, generous lady. It was a Friday night and her house was full of activity, visitors, cousins, and noise. I explained to her what had just happened. She was very supportive and showed me to a lovely bedroom where I could stay. The dogs were taken to the basement recreational room to play with their dogs, which were also Doberman Pinschers.

I sat on the bed, thinking about what I had just accomplished, and staring at the walls. Overcome with anxiety, despair, and confusion, I began sobbing. When I could sob no more, feeling exhausted and weak, I opened my Bible and began talking aloud to the Lord, asking him to take me away from all of this. That definitely wasn't his plan. I then realized that to continue on, I would need His guidance and protection; most of all, His protection. I would need a lot of protection. I began to read aloud the 23rd Psalm:

"The Lord is my Shepherd I shall not want.
He makes me lie down in green pastures;
He leads me beside quiet waters,
He restores my soul;
He guides me in the paths of righteousness,
For His name's sake.
Even though I walk through the valley of the shadow of death,
I fear no evil; for Thou art with me;
Thy rod and Thy staff, they comfort me.
Thou dost prepare a table before me in the presence of my enemies;
Thou hast anointed my head with oil;
My cup overflows.
Surely goodness and loving kindness
will follow me all the days of my life,
And I will dwell in the house of the Lord forever."

I also began reading aloud Psalm 25, *A Psalm of David:*
"To Thee, O Lord, I lift up my soul.
O my God, in Thee I trust.
Do not let me be ashamed;
Do not let my enemies exult over me.
Indeed, none of those who wait for Thee will be ashamed;
Those who deal treacherously without cause will be ashamed.
Make me know thy ways, O Lord;
Teach me Thy paths. Lead me in Thy truth and teach me,
For Thou art the God of my salvation;
For Thee I wait all the day.
Remember, O Lord,
Thy compassion and Thy loving kindnesses,
for they have been from of old.
Do not remember the sins of my youth or my transgressions;
According to Thy loving kindness remember Thou me,
For Thy goodness sake, O Lord.
Good and upright is the Lord;
Therefore he instructs sinners in the way.
He leads the humble in justice,
and He teaches the humble His way."

I prayed hard that night and slept with my Bible on my heart. When I awakened, I was disoriented by my new surroundings, wondering whether my reality was a dream, or my dream a reality. In spite of my mental haziness, I had a strong, new sense of hope and protection. Finally, I felt I was not alone. I arose from the bed, committed to following God's way. Little did I know that this newfound faith would be the turning point of my life.

Renting Rooms

I left my ex-husband in March 1988. Almost every morning since then, I awakened with a gentle observance of my new and different surroundings. Absorbing this new situation created a gradual, heavy, sinking feeling in my stomach that grew from the mild internal struggle of my new, uncertain life. Each day, I was faced with the challenge of having to carve out something new for myself. I no longer lived with my familiar situation—my abuser and his violence. It was a volatile situation which had blended so well with my programmed needs.

Strangely, I did not feel really happy about my liberation. I had left the comfortable familiarity of a predictable and known situation. Although it was a horrible situation, I still had the strange comfort of knowing my enemy's routine and behavior. It seemed much harder to adapt to a new living situation in which I had to re-think and re-create my days. There was no convenient distraction to focus all of my energies toward. I was no longer consumed with "out-guessing" my opponent or managing that certain domestic chaos. Now, I had to focus on the unknown and me.

In an effort to delay this deep inward reflection, I just muddled through my day, going through the basic routine of keeping up the professional façade at work, taking aerobic classes at the gym, and looking for a more permanent and affordable place to live. I went through the daily motions of any professional woman, just to appear functional. However, deep inside, I was watching life from the sideline, feeling distant, disengaged and removed from my own divine power. I was fully engaged in the satisfaction and comfort of being a victim and still feeling sorry for myself.

In spring 1988, Easter Sunday was approaching and I had made a promise to God to honor and devote my life to obeying Him. Struggling to maintain this commitment and to practice some degree of faith, I attended a church service on Palm Sunday. I did not regret it. Being at church on that Sunday morning was a glorious event. I felt that God, my Guardian Angels, my Mom, and my Grandmother were all there with me in the church, sitting next to me. I felt their warm and powerful embraces all around me. I sang with deep feeling, as tears rolled down my cheeks, ruining my well-placed mascara and eye-liner make-up.

When I left the service, I carried my palm with me to my car and placed it carefully on the dashboard as a symbol of my hope and protection. It remained there for 12 years, removed only once when I traded in the Blazer in 1999.

Days passed as I tried to keep up mentally, emotionally and spiritually. After about two months, I realized I needed to find a different place to live since I had no privacy with everyone in the house; more importantly, I was obsessively worried and anxious about Doug finding me. It would be only a matter of time until he did, and I yearned for my own safe space where I could move about freely, openly and safely.

I worried obsessively about Doug finding me. Whenever I tried to relax a little, I found my thoughts racing, always focused on him. I didn't know whether or not he would suddenly appear at my friend's door, and I feared that if he did, she would nonchalantly allow him to enter because she was so welcoming to others and confident that she could handle any type of situation. I knew she wouldn't be able to handle him and worried obsessively about this imagined event. I knew I would have to leave and find another place to stay, one hidden from acquaintances and the possibility of him ever finding me.

I scoured the newspapers, searching for a place that would accept me and my two dogs. I found a room to rent in Landover, MD, in a cute townhouse owned by a "no nonsense" Black woman. She was a few years older than me, probably in her late thirties, and was all about her business of renting the room, with little time for small talk. I could sense she had been through her own battles in life as I gently searched her countenance for compassion. Her attractive, chocolate-brown face was full of unforgiven events. She was uninterested in hearing the facts about my circumstance and showed no sympathy towards me. She laid down the rules immediately: rent was to be paid on time, no visitors, no pets, and clean up after yourself in the kitchen.

My room was very small, very hot and seemed to be drowning in a deep forest green. The carpet, bedspread and walls were all dark green—a strange color for a bedroom. The other tenant, a Black guy in his late forties, had a brown room. I was introduced to him when I was given a brief tour of the house but I had no interest in getting to know him or any guy.

I settled into my surroundings after about two weeks, reminding myself often that this was only a temporary situation. I strongly believed and imagined I would have my own place to live in someday, somewhere, once I had dug myself out of this marriage debacle. Having my own place was a vivid dream, far off into the future. An aching but vivid dream, overshadowed by a monster for a husband, mortgage payments, expensive attorney fees, my dogs now in the kennel, the search for a new job and my strained effort to keep my sanity.

In between brief, expensive meetings with my attorney, I visited my dogs at the kennel in Maryland. It was owned and operated by a wonderful, kind woman, who was blonde and in her fifties. She was soft spoken, with kind eyes and a loving spirit, and I could tell she loved animals a lot by the way she described her struggling business and what she did for the dogs. Her kennel business was on a few acres of fenced-in property, with many old cages. In spite of her struggles with the business, she was very kind and eager to help me. She listened sympathetically to my plight and told me she would take good care of my dogs.

I eagerly paid the monthly fees, knowing that my dogs would be receiving loving treatment. I knew I'd be able to be with them soon, once I found a place to live that would accept pets. I visited them almost every day and loved looking at their smiles when they greeted me. We played catch and wrestled in the grass together. When my visit was over, I drove back to the rented room, crying to fill the huge emptiness and searing pain in my gut from having to leave my best friends. My face formed its familiar stretching as I sobbed loudly all the way home, receiving strange looks from nearby drivers.

Although I was broken about having to leave my dogs at the kennel, I was grateful for the woman at the kennel who was helping me. She had listened to my story and was an angel to me. She was full of "light" and radiated kindness. She demonstrated a deep compassion towards me that I had never experienced from a stranger. She was someone who seemed to take my hand and guide me through my trouble, instructing me not to worry.

She quickly understood how much I loved my dogs and what I had experienced in my brief marriage. She understood how horrid my situation had been and, when I was low on cash, she understood with compassion and waited for my payments. In my quiet moments, I thought about her kindness that was so foreign to me. I was amazed and in awe about her spirit and who she was. Her devotion to animals and her willingness to help a total stranger were like miracles. She impressed upon me how important it is to help others in this journey called life. I decided from that day forward, I would some day help someone in dire need, as she had helped me.

A New Job

I considered locating a good kennel a big achievement. My next obstacle to overcome was to find a new place to work. This would be a challenge. I wanted to leave the Navy Research Center for two reasons. First, Doug would be able to find me easily if I stayed at my current place of work; second, I was not advancing quickly.

Although I had regained my Grade 12 status, after losing it from the previous RIF (lay-off), all the "signs" were telling me that I would not advance any further. The final blow came when I was asked to train an older Caucasian male for the Grade 13 position in our office, for which I knew I was well-qualified.

"Yes, it's time to leave," I thought. Whether it was my ambitious style at work, the organization's culture, my lack of networking skills, or my brief years at the Center, there was an unstated reason why I was not being considered for the next higher grade level. I think it was because the Center's culture could not embrace the vision of a young, capable Black woman having the same grade level and position as more "mature" Caucasian males, who had been there for over 20 years. I had firmly decided I was not going to hang around for another 20 years to receive just one promotion!

This situation was another one of my disappointing lessons about justice, merit, hard work and fairness. I had believed that, if I worked really hard and produced high quality work, I would automatically progress up the corporate ladder quickly like others. I thought I had been fully accepted, regardless of my race or gender. I slowly realized that in spite of all the hard work or my credentials, I was never going to "fit in" and had hit the glass ceiling.

When I unguardedly shared this disappointing situation with a new colleague who was doing some consulting work for the organization, he understood and wanted to help me. I was pleasantly surprised by this reception. He was an older Caucasian male who had a good solid political network. He was aware of a possible opportunity in another organization and, later that month, he asked for my resume. I forwarded my resume and, after about a few months, went through an application process. I did a great interview and within several weeks, I was hired.

I was so happy and grateful about this connection and it forced me to reassess my resentment about the "white establishment." I knew I couldn't be angry or categorically opposed to all Caucasians, because this man had helped me. I was learning there are so many kind people willing to help along the way and I couldn't hold on to my learned, racist viewpoints. I was beginning to value each individual's merit, not the race they belonged to.

I loved my new job. It involved traveling, quality training, and innovation—my three favorite things! With this new position and the probability that Doug would never find me, I started to feel as if I was gaining some control over my situation. I felt hopeful and it was great! Now, all I had to contend with was keeping the dogs well-cared for, paying the bills, and tolerating the constant pestering from the landlady where I had rented the room. She had started to nag me about the pubic hairs on the bathroom floor. Where else could pubic hairs go? It was a ridiculous situation.

The Call from Hank

Needless to say, my family members were very concerned about me. I was still trying to maintain the phony façade that I was handling my life well. They called often, and I shared very little about how I was really feeling, how helpless I felt. One evening, my oldest brother, Hank, called. I couldn't hold back any longer and began pouring my heart out to him. I described the bad situation I was in and in between sobs, I told him what a failure I was. I described how bad my finances were, and how I had totally screwed up my life. I told him I wanted to kill myself and cried hard, loud and long. I could hear his sniffling at the other end of the phone, which was an unusual display of emotion for him because we'd always tease him about his lack of compassion and his "just the facts" attitude. Now, he was crying, too, and I was really moved by his sympathy.

When we both got control of our tears and sniffles, I explained my finances in detail to him, my income and how my money was being spent. After listening carefully, he got serious with me and said the dreadful, but anticipated, words to me, "Gina, you're going to have to give up the dogs."

I started crying again and told him the dogs were all I had and that they were my only true friends. I tried to convince him I could manage the high cost of the kennel, the mortgage, and the other bills. He said sternly, "If you want to get some control of your money and move out of the rented room, it's your only option."

I thought, "Shit, who wants to make this choice?"

After our conversation, I knew he was right but my heart was aching. My dogs! They were all I had left. I mentally chose to block out what Doug had probably done to my pets. I couldn't handle those thoughts. All I could think about was keeping my dogs, so I discussed this situation with the kennel owner, who also felt it was the right thing for me to do. She assured me she could easily find a good home for my nice, well-behaved dogs. She promised me and she kept her promise. They were adopted by a couple who were expecting a baby. The husband traveled often and wanted some good dogs to help guard his wife. That was a happy solution—a good, happy ending.

My brother Hank really stayed with me emotionally and supported me throughout my ordeal. He wanted me to keep up my faith and called me often because he was very worried about me. He loaned me about $2,000 (a huge amount in 1989) to clean up some bills that were delinquent. He also took a lot of time to record smooth jazz music and encouraging self-help tapes and messages for me. He mailed newly recorded music on cassette tapes and sent me numerous "positive thinking" and "creating a successful attitude" tapes to listen to. He was a sales manager, and many of his professional tapes were copied and mailed to me. I really appreciated his thoughtfulness and caring.

I listened to those tapes constantly and absorbed everything they were saying. I was an eager student, intent on learning new ways to help myself succeed. I was adamant about reshaping my life and began to learn how to visualize, how to keep a positive attitude and how to demonstrate persistence. I listened to my "positive attitude" tapes at home and in the car. It was good to hear stories of how other people faced numerous hardships and overcame them with a positive attitude and persistence—people such as Abraham Lincoln, George Washington Carver and others who believed they could do it! My brother really helped me by sharing these cassette tapes with me, and he became a good friend as well as the best big brother a girl could have. I was glad I had poured out my heart to him because I received a new gift from him. He believed in *me*.

The Accident or "The Law of Attraction"

My new job was going well, but staying in the green rented room was getting the better of me, and it was harder to endure the weekends. Getting through the week was easy because I could lose myself in my new job with lots of hard work. I was a workaholic and eager to excel. The harder I worked, the less I had to think about my personal life. At work, I never talked about my physical abuse or where I was living. It was my big secret. But I hated my weekends.

When Fridays came, I eagerly planned an event to delay my arrival to the "green room." I looked forward to a party or some other social event so that I could have a drink and forget about the pain of my situation. I was not interested in meeting someone new or any dating; I just wanted to have a good drink. I loved White Russians, Margaritas, and anything else with tequila.

One Friday night, I overdid the drinking. I went to a bar with some new girlfriends, and eventually consumed three tequila sunrises. While we were drinking, we were criticizing and wishing negative thoughts about men. I had some special, private thoughts about my soon-to-be ex-husband. I had wished he was in a car accident! Yes, I really wanted him to be gone from the face of the earth and wished intently for a car accident to happen to him.

Somehow, in spite of the drinks, I managed to drive the car and arrived home safely. While getting dressed for bed, I saw my depressing note about an 11:00 a.m. appointment with my attorney on Saturday morning. I set my alarm clock for 9:30 and stumbled into bed. I slept hard and awakened to shrill music from the radio. I felt a little nauseous and dressed sloppily and hurriedly. While climbing into the Blazer, I was still wishing for a bad accident to happen to Doug. I drove mindlessly down Landover Road, when suddenly the car in front of me seemed to come closer and closer, as if in slow motion and smashed into the front of my car. The car behind me rear-ended me, and the car behind that car rear-ended it. A four-car crash all because I had failed to apply my brakes quickly enough.

We all got out of our cars, observed the damage and collectively used a few choice expletives. While waiting for the police, we exchanged names, phone numbers and insurance information. I introduced myself to the others and apologized profusely, feeling the blame from everyone. I explained that I was going through a divorce and was not my usual self. Everyone seemed to understand immediately.

There's something about using the "divorce" word in that many people seem to understand about the divorce hardship thing. It's as if I became a privileged member of a certain Pain Club or something. I didn't question it too much but was just grateful for the understanding.

I called to notify my attorney about my delay, and we set up our appointment for later that same day. I appreciated his understanding, but regretted the likely double billing that would occur for that day; even phone calls were billed! Later, while driving to his office, I thought about what I had just experienced and had a revelation. I saw how I had attracted that accident to myself by being so busy wishing for an accident for husband that I brought one upon myself.

This lesson was powerful and transformative for me. During that moment of clarity, I received an insight about the power of my own thoughts in creating what happens to me. It was a scary thought for someone who often felt helpless and victimized. It was difficult for me to believe, at that time, that I could create my situation. That I was ultimately responsible for what happened to me! This was my first experience with a natural law:

"We attract to ourselves what we hold in our minds."

This was an example of the Natural Law of Attraction, a principle that would later become the cornerstone of my life.

Restraining Orders!

During Saturday's appointment with my attorney, I signed the draft divorce papers and was told quite candidly that it would be best to sell the house. I didn't want to hear this and told him I was still paying the mortgage so I could move back in. He told me that since both names were on the title deed, we would have to sell it and then divide any proceeds. Then he paused and added, "Unless he, your husband, wants to buy you out and stay on the property."

I despised him for even thinking of this as an alternative. Then I thought about how impossible that would be for Doug, or that maybe it was a joke because my husband had never paid a mortgage note in his life, never having earned any money on a consistent basis.

I left the attorney's office emotionally upset as usual. After much reflection and anger, I later agreed to discontinue paying the mortgage notes so that the house could be sold. After making this monumental decision, I thought that the divorce situation was soon coming to an end. The house could quickly be sold and I would be a free woman, no longer being tied to my husband. I was wrong. It was only a different beginning. Months later, I found out from my attorney that Doug had continued to live in the home but was refusing to pay the bills, including the mortgage note. On hearing this, I became sick to my stomach. Was Doug doing all of this just to spite me? Was he still thinking that I would return? I grimaced at the thought of his insane trickery.

My attorney said that Doug would have to be removed from the home and we'd have to foreclose on it eventually if he continued to ignore the mortgage payments! I felt that Doug was either anticipating my return or trying very hard to ruin my excellent credit rating. Or maybe both. At some point, I would have to go back to gather my belongings and some furniture but dreaded the thought of having to face him again. I knew I would need a police escort, so these arrangements were made, and I went to my home with police escorts a few weeks later.

To my surprise, many of my personal items were gone. I was unable to find my personal diary, some sentimental pictures and other precious personal items. I did however, locate my precious Raggedy Ann doll and happily carried her to the car. The furniture that was left was packed and placed in a storage facility. My heart was heavy with sad thoughts of what could have been ... if things had been positive.

During this divorce, I had the opportunity to discover the hard way that nothing is ever rational between a man and a woman during a contentious divorce process. My soon-to-be ex-husband was not trying to cooperate in any way. Over several months, he repeatedly ignored the court appointments for our divorce hearings in Upper Marlboro, Maryland, and he refused to pay any mortgage payments. The saga over the house foreclosure dragged on for two more years, because he suddenly started to pay some mortgage payments. I wondered where and how he obtained the money, and speculated that he was probably selling drugs to make the payments because he hated working a "nine-to-five" job.

The sporadic mortgage payments caused further delays and complications in the foreclosure process. The "house situation" was an albatross around my neck which I could not loosen. I had no control or influence during this suffocating divorce process as Doug was desperately holding on to whatever control he could, and my spirit could not escape his far-reaching grasp.

In spite of the threat of another restraining order, he started to call me at my new job, begging me to come back to him. He called every day, several times a day. On some days, he would call ten or twenty times repeatedly, in the span of an hour, causing my co-workers to look at me oddly and wonder what was happening. One time, he called me to tell me that my pet turtles were dead. He knew how much I loved my pets and he used this line to try to get me back into the house, knowing I would try to rescue my bunny.

Often I would try to not answer the telephone on my desk. When I didn't answer the phone, it would ring and ring for an hour or more.

Since we were all separated only by partitions at work, everyone seemed to know I had some type of problem. Although I felt ashamed, embarrassed and trapped, I tried to act as if it was nothing. I was still trying to keep up the façade, the professional appearance but managing this façade and the lingering trauma took a lot of energy.

I couldn't figure out who might have given him my new office phone number. Did I make another mistake? Did I trust an acquaintance too much? Or did my contacts at the old job innocently give him my new work number? Now I had another dangerous problem to solve. I told my attorney I might need another stronger restraining order, since Doug was not getting the message that our relationship had ended. I was afraid and told my attorney that he was going to try to kill me. He had made serious promises about it in the past and I believed him, so my attorney instructed me to call the police whenever I saw him and to be watchful.

Being watchful was not a problem as I was already hyper-vigilant and overly anxious. Whenever I walked outside, I always looked for the nearest telephone. I watched people behind me, always looking back over my shoulder to see if I was being followed. I envisioned different escape scenarios so I could be ready in the event he jumped out of a bush or tried to gag me again. Every small, dark Black man with a beard was my potential assailant.

While walking home, I would sigh with relief whenever I saw police cars or police officers. With their presence, maybe I'd be safe. I wanted to feel safe and protected. It had been a long time since I'd felt protected and guarded by love. I was angry at my ex-husband and I hated the prison he had locked me in. Fear was all I knew.

Post-Traumatic Stress Disorder

Living in fear and horror for many months took its toll on me psychologically. I was afraid and startled by many things, including strangers, and I worked hard to protect myself. I promised myself that no one was *ever* going to get close to me again. I was going to keep people at a distance, or at least be in total control. I avoided situations that made me feel helpless or insignificant.

Whenever I could, I did my daily exercises using my Jane Fonda videotape or jogging around the neighborhood park. I wanted to improve my exercise program and had hoped to join a gym someday, to participate in aerobic classes. Exercising helped me escape from my reality and made me feel beautiful and capable of having some control over my life. I loved to exercise, for it made me feel good for a while, and the endorphins made me feel invincible.

At work, I continued to excel and tried to be a perfectionist. I was very critical of myself and rarely felt good about any of my accomplishments. When I did achieve something, I would always immediately set my sights for the next challenge. Overcoming challenges at work was thrilling and satisfying to me, and helped build my confidence.

I spent a lot of time either trying to forget the past or focus on the future. I set a lot of future goals, one right after the other, and did not like living in the moment. My reactions to real-time events were usually delayed responses. When events happened, such as interpersonal incidents at work, I would later perform "self-talk" about how I should have or could have done or said something differently, well after the situation had passed. I had not lived "in the moment" for a long time.

Over the years, I had learned well how to shield myself from the chaos, the fighting and the abuse by "tuning-out" or disassociating myself. I stayed "tuned out" or in a daze to keep from being in the present moment because being "in the moment" was far too painful. Detachment was better, and my obsessive behaviors helped me to stay detached and in denial about my pain. I was obsessive about my exercise routine, my work and my daily habits, to avoid remembering the past or to avoid being in the present.

I rarely relaxed without a drink. I enjoyed "social drinking" because it was my escape from my pain. Natural relaxation was foreign to me and I wanted to keep it that way. My good, pain-free moments were all derived from "doing" and achieving, not from just "being." I felt I was only as good as my next achievement.

I was totally unaware of how messed up I was, and was certain no one could see through my professional façade but I was wrong. One person did see through the pretense and self-protection. He was Kyle, an employee who worked with me. We first started talking regularly about our work activities. We would share new ideas about our approaches for reaching goals and would criticize and make jokes about our boss. Kyle had a great sense of humor and made me laugh a lot. He was a kind person and a good listener, who I felt safe talking with. Even when he was on the receiving end of my moodiness, my anger or my irrational thinking, he never criticized me. Instead, he did make me think about my behaviors with his gentle questioning.

Almost everyday, after one of our conversations, he would leave me with something to think about. We had some really deep, reflective dialogues about relationships, psychology, race, religion, health, homosexuality, families, physical abuse, careers, finances, restaurants and mysticism. We developed a strong emotional bond over a three-year period. He generously shared his progressive ideas, instructional guidance and sensitive emotions with me, and he seemed to mirror my own quest for learning.

Often, after work, we would stop to get a bite to eat at the local snack shop or at a fine restaurant. I learned about different cuisine, new restaurants and fine wine. He was a very tall, lean man and I was of medium height. When we walked home together, up towards Dupont Circle, I bet we looked like Sesame Street's Big Bird and Chicken Little. Needless to say, he became my best friend, another "angel" sent my way to protect me, support me and to help me grow.

When I wasn't on the job, or exercising or talking to Kyle, I was doing my best to avoid any painful reminders about my marriage and divorce process. When I watched television, any images of violence stayed stuck in my mind, especially if the violence was toward women. When I watched sentimental and poignant movies, I was incapable of crying. I was numb, dazed, and indifferent and could not feel any delicate, tender emotions.

To prevent panic attacks or triggers, I avoided parts of the city that reminded me of Doug. I even developed a dislike for certain foods I used to eat with him. Anxiety triggers were everywhere—a romantic song, a person's appearance, a piece of clothing, the telephone ringing, going to retrieve my daily mail—all triggered heart palpitations and shortness of breath.

When I could, I avoided answering the telephone, afraid it might be Doug. I avoided going to the post office box for fear I would have more overdue bills to pay. There were so many of these anxiety triggers that I found myself trying so hard to control and manage them, which left very little energy for doing a lot of interpersonal relating to others. When I did attempt to interact with others, I showed no patience or understanding. My motto at that time was: "Get on with it," or, "Cut to the chase." I balanced my inner world of trauma with my outer world of daily existence ... and it was exhausting.

Hatred

I hated my soon-to-be ex-husband for what he had done to me. My pain had me slowly begin to hate all Black men. On the street, I never made any eye contact with a Black man as he walked towards me. In fact, as soon as I discovered he wasn't Doug, I would quickly avert my glance to another direction. If he wasn't Doug, he was invisible to me. When they weren't invisible, I despised them. I decided all the hype about Black men was just that—so much hype. They became all a bunch of empty, macho images.

From my experiences, I knew them as lousy, lying lovers, irresponsible, crude and financially inadequate dicks on a stick. When I did see or learn of a Black man going about his life responsibly, overcoming obstacles and achieving goals, I thought to myself, here's a "Wonder Boy" who probably despises Black women. There was nothing any Black man could do or say to shift my attitude towards him, at that time. I even wrote poems about how much I disliked them.

I had a special saying about Doug, which I found in some article or book. Every time I read it or thought about it, I just laughed and laughed until tears formed in my eyes. I really hated him. Here's the saying I found one day:

**"Help Wanted
A small Black Man to be a Mud Flap.
Must be flexible and willing to travel."**

Doug was a skinny, small Black man and this saying gave me much joy as I read it. I had chosen to never date or marry another Black man. I was finished with the whole lot. If I were to date again, I had planned to broaden my horizons and to drop any cultural loyalty I had towards the Black man. My hatred was palpable and I was drowning in it.

The Sanctuary

I spent my Saturdays away from the "green room," searching the newspapers for a nicer place to live. I really wanted to live in a pretty apartment and somehow I would figure out a way to have it. Sadly, I knew my credit rating was probably taking a nose dive by this time, but at least I was making some decent money. I was grateful for my steady income and I thanked God I'd listened to my mother's direction about getting a good education. It was my ticket to independence and maybe a better life.

I had noticed that most, if not all, the problems I saw among Black folks were the results of a poor education. I was proud that I had stuck it out and finished a Master of Public Administration degree. It wasn't easy. I recalled existing on only peanut butter sandwiches and locking myself in for the weekend to finish writing school papers during beautiful spring days. For a minute, I felt like my own hero.

Eventually, my searching the newspapers led me to the heavenly ad: "Newly renovated, charming 1 bedroom apartment with fireplace, balcony, walk to downtown, $850/month." My heart skipped a beat because I loved fireplaces. Also, it was near downtown where I worked and seemed affordable. I just knew it would be mine and immediately called the landlord to set up an appointment to see the apartment.

The next Tuesday, I took an early lunch break and left my office building to arrive at the noon appointment on time. On the way, I rehearsed the interview in my mind. I was going to be forthright, even at great risk of losing the apartment. I felt I had no choice but to be honest about everything. I knew I had to reveal my divorce situation and my poor credit rating to the potential landlord.

I approached Swann Street and stopped at the corner to look down the street. It was a lovely, picturesque street with brownstones on each side, shaded by mature Ginko trees. Pleased with what I saw, I walked more quickly down the street and arrived at a nice, well-maintained red-brick building. The apartment was a walk-up, on the second floor. At the top of the stairs, I shyly knocked at the partially opened door and a man's voice asked me to enter.

A dapper, older Caucasian man reached out to shake my hand. He had an aura of health, wealth and worldliness. He showed me around the tiny apartment, consisting of a modern bathroom and a kitchenette with new tile flooring, new carpeting throughout, a fireplace and a nice-sized bedroom with French doors leading to a cute balcony with a sliding glass door. The sliding door was the only source of sunlight over the entire apartment, but it was just enough. I really loved the apartment!

We sat down at the kitchen table and had a long conversation. I was honest and candid. I told him about my situation, my credit and my salary. I completed the application and offered references. I was eager to make this place my new home. When our talk was finished, we shook hands and he said he would call me the next day with his decision. Tomorrow seemed so far off; I didn't think I could wait that long.

I walked back to the office dreaming about how wonderful it would be to live there. I visualized myself living there, sitting by the fire, feeling protected and safe from Doug. The building had good security so I would really be safe. I prayed and prayed about getting the apartment but worried about my credit rating interspersed with hateful thoughts of my husband once again. Finally, I stopped worrying and told God, "If You want me to be there, I will be. I leave it in Your hands."

The next day at work, I hovered over the telephone. I had described the apartment to Kyle and he was keeping his fingers crossed for me. I couldn't eat or concentrate on my work, so I just stared at the phone, willing it to ring. When it did, it was Doug and I quickly hung up. I already knew what he was going to do—make new threats toward me because of his anger over the restraining order he had just received.

The phone rang again. I took a deep breath and answered it, not knowing who would be on the other end. It was the landlord telling me that I was the new tenant! I was ecstatic and thanked him effusively, already making plans to give notice to the landlady of the "green room." The following day, I scheduled a mover to retrieve my furniture from the storage facility and delivered a hefty security deposit to the landlord. I thanked him again and I silently thanked God. I felt very fortunate and thought, "Yes, honesty really is the best policy."

Three weeks later, I moved into my new dream apartment feeling as if I'd died and gone to heaven! It was more beautiful than I had remembered and it became my fortress with privacy. People had to be buzzed in to this quiet, clean building of only three apartments, of which mine was the smallest and the cutest!

I didn't have much furniture at the time—two wicker chairs, a rocker and an ottoman. I put Raggedy Ann on the fireplace mantle, and slept on the floor for many nights. When Kyle heard this, he gave me a futon he didn't need, and it felt like sleeping on a cloud after the hard floor. A month later my landlord sold me a big, beautiful brass bed, fit for a queen. In fact, I began to feel like a queen in her private tower. I felt safe and that this was going to be my sanctuary, safe from evil and closer to God.

The Monster on the Door

It took a few months to set up the apartment to match my dream. I put sheer curtains at the windows to encourage the sunlight to enter. I bought new kitchen utensils, a huge comforter and pillows for my new bed and pictures for the walls. I loved being there in my safe space, all on my own. However, at night, I still had nightmares about Doug finding me and other strange dreams from which I would often awaken sweating in fear. I would jump out of bed to check the locks on the doors and the balcony window one more time.

One night, I remember looking at the natural design of the wood on the back of my oak door and vividly saw the face of an evil monster in the design. I told myself it was only the design of the wood grain, but it didn't matter. I still saw the face of a monster. Obviously, I was still living in fear, in spite of my soft, protective surroundings.

I wanted to be my own hero and didn't like living in fear. It made me feel small, unworthy and powerless, and I knew I had to do something more to remove the fear permeating my every thought. I began to think warm thoughts about my Mom and my Grandmother. Usually, they slipped into my dreams and I would often wake crying because I missed them so much. I wanted them to see my new apartment and to be proud of me.

I fondly remembered how my Grandmother would drink Maxwell House coffee each morning as she read her *Daily Word* booklet which was full of Bible verses for the month. To get closer to her, I bought a coffee-maker and a subscription to the *Daily Word*. As I read the passages each day, I was comforted by her presence and by His presence. And, although my days became a little calmer, I was still living with big-time fear and anxiety, constantly still afraid, like a scared little mouse. I felt as if everything was out to get me and trusted no one. Fear dominated my existence and I was living in a small box.

Reshaping My Life

In spite of a frustrating day at work, I joyfully walked home, eager to arrive at my new, safe home and sanctuary. That day, I had the courage to stop at the mailbox before going upstairs. Going to the mailbox and opening up the mail was an experience still filled with anxiety. As I grabbed the mail, my heart palpitated and my breathing changed to short pants. I had six bills and one personal letter and anxiously worried if there would be a new bill created by Doug, maybe an overdraft bank notice, a "second notice" credit card bill or a letter from the kennel. I ignored the bills and opened the letter; it was from my father.

He must have found out about my situation from Hank. I could only imagine that he was going to chastise me for being stupid and stubborn but I read the letter over and over again because there was no "I told you so" or any self-righteousness. I could hardly believe the encouraging and kind words from my father: "Hello Gina. I hope you are doing better. I found out about your situation from your brother. Please do not worry. Remember that with time, this too shall pass. Now be brave, stout-hearted and courageous."

I stood in the hallway and allowed his words to cuddle me. I thought long and hard about what it might mean to be brave, stout-hearted and courageous. I guessed it meant being my own hero.

How was I ever going to save myself? How was I ever going to dig out from under a mountain of bills? How was I ever going to improve my poor credit rating? How long would it take? Where do I start? As these questions circled my head constantly, I continued to work out at a new exercise club, Spa Lady, which helped me assemble some control over my life. I would walk home from work, exhausted, mildly confident and reflective. When I wasn't anxiously scoping the streets for Doug, I dreamed a lot about what my new life would look like. I thought about having nice clothes, a new home just for me and having no debt!

When I arrived home, my usual ritual consisted of quickly stripping down and running hot water for a good delicious bubble bath.

I'd grab a favorite book to read as my muscles said, "Ahhhh" when I sank into the water. At the time I was reading *Co-Dependent No More* by Melody Beattie. I devoured this book that seemed to be just what I needed. It helped me to uncover some subconscious, destructive relationship patterns I had not realized I was locked into. I learned a method for understanding and analyzing my past, and how it had shaped my relationships.

The book described a pattern common for many people, not just me. It helped me unlearn some relationship habits based on feelings of shame. Receiving strong physical discipline as a child had instilled deep feelings of worthlessness and shame. I was super sensitive as a child and everything affected me in a traumatic fashion. I began to understand me and take my first step towards a more healthy way of seeing things, of seeing me. It felt like a first step towards my own recovery.

Setting Goals

That weekend, I made a firm decision to begin improving my life in some way. I had to start somewhere and strongly believed that this life was the only one I had. I knew it was not a dress rehearsal for my "real" life, and wanted to be the star of my own show. I thought about Dad's words, "Be brave" and really felt and believed I had his full support for the first time in my life. I always knew him as a courageous man, somewhat volatile, but always courageous and thought I could be like him in that way, so I started to act courageously.

I sat at my kitchen table with a pen and pad of paper and began to list some goals. At first, it seemed as if I was just playing around, but, after working with the words, the exercise of actually writing the goals down on paper became more possible and real in my mind. I started to enjoy it and wrote a lot of goals, one for each catastrophic area of my life. Most everything was broken except my career, so I established financial, psychological, spiritual, and career goals.

For the first year, 1988, I started with carving out some financial goals. The second year, 1989, was for my mental health or psychological wellness goals. The third year, 1990, was for my spiritual goals, which really continued for many years since I had to explore my spiritual self and slowly build towards self-mastery. I re-shaped and revised the career goals, but realized career goals had to be last because I knew I couldn't sustain an outstanding career if my mental, emotional and spiritual selves were unbalanced and shallow.

The financial goal was the most immediate, since I had attorney fees, kennel fees and bad credit. I knew I was going to continue to have bad credit until the house situation was resolved. Doug had continued to stay in the house as he struggled with the mortgage payments. His financial failures became my failures because my name was still on the property title, so any late or missed payments were black marks against me, as well. It was agonizing and I cried a lot about this situation. However, after a few months, I stopped crying and worrying about it, and began to accept it for what it was. Looking forward, I vowed to never co-sign any property with a man. Never, ever.

I began to focus on what was within my own control. I paid off all the credit cards and vowed to never be late with any bills or payments in my name. I planned a budget and stuck with it. After one year of this good behavior, I tried to maximize my take-home (net) pay by consulting with a Certified Public Accountant, who advised me to withhold more money from my federal taxes.

This great advice helped for a while, until the next year in April, when I received a notice from the IRS telling me I owed the United States Treasury about $1,500! I was stunned, scared and then angry. Here I was, trying to help a professional "Brother" to whom I'd been referred but ended up being swindled. He had given me some bad tax advice, creating yet another new situation which I could angrily add to my "I Hate Black Men" inventory.

I slowly read the notice again and again with hands trembling with fear. I just did not want to deal with the IRS at this time, so I defiantly shoved the letter into my top drawer and slammed it shut. I was tired of being harassed and thought, "Out of sight, out of mind."

Denial and Defense

I did not want to be hurt by anyone anymore, whether it was the IRS, men, strangers on the street, my boss or any other authority figure. I didn't care who or what it was, and just wanted the pain to stop. I crept back into my denial that I'd ever received the IRS notice. While walking home from work, I bought a lovely white dress I thought Cinderella or Snow White might have worn. It made me feel very special, like a fairy-tale princess.

Spending money on me to make myself feel good was a strange act for me. I was only familiar with spending money to pay bills, taking care of obligations, or buying a gift for someone else. However, once I got over the strange sensation of buying for me, I was eager to slide into the nice feeling of it, and stayed there. It felt really great to spend money on me and eased the pain I was feeling all the time, taking me to another pleasant world. I thought, "I'll deal with the IRS later. Right now, I need dresses," and bought a new summer dress almost every other week. The denial I lived in was exciting and comforting.

During those days, I was also learning to protect myself in every way, with almost anyone. I seemed to have gone to the other extreme and tried to defend myself when there was no need to. I even threatened to punch my dentist in the stomach as if he had *planned* to hurt me during a wisdom tooth extraction. I teetered between vulnerable high anxiety and a formidable defensive posture. There was no middle ground or equanimity, and I became a volatile, moody Black woman … and I was still only in my early thirties!

I knew something had to change. I needed to change … on the inside. I had to make a conscious choice to either stay in my self-righteous anger and limiting fear, or grow into a better person. I wanted to get back to the lovable core I remembered myself being—a kind, gentle, loving woman who would care for anyone or anything. I missed who I used to be, the "nice Gina." I felt robbed of my personality, as if my real self had just walked away from me without looking back.

Back to Church

Something deep down was gnawing at me to keep moving forward. I thought a little about going back to church, but the few thoughts I had about church weren't very pleasant. I had bad childhood memories of church and the people in it—hypocrites, liars and cheats. I remembered people professing being Christian, but who really attended church to rid themselves of the guilt they felt from their sins committed during the other six days of the week. I saw no integrity there, just ministers who were not professionals and talked one way but acted in another.

I disliked the thought of going into a building on Sundays to hear a man in the pulpit talk about how he thinks God wants me to behave and will judge me if I don't. I had no faith in someone else's interpretation of the Bible and wanted to explore my own very personal relationship with God, *my* God, who was a God full of compassion, kindness and understanding.

I still prayed every morning before leaving the house and I often talked to God. I enjoyed reading my *Daily Word* over coffee because it felt like my Grandmother was right there beside me, reading it with me. I had often asked God to guide and forgive me for my bad choices and occasional swearing. As I started to enjoy my private relationship with God, I was still sorting things out and visualizing what He was to me. I did not profess or brag about my Christianity or my relationship with the Lord.

Whenever someone would ask about the church I belonged to, I would respond with how much I disliked organized religion and how I wanted to strengthen my own spirituality. Somehow there just seemed to be a bit more latitude with claiming my spirituality rather than my religion. It allowed for different perspectives and varied definitions, and it gave me time to think things through and decide what was relevant and important *for me.*

I saw spirituality as an individual, personal quest for my own God-self, not to be shaped by outsiders who dictated on Sundays what was best for me. I was open to learning new ways of building and strengthening my own very personal relationship to God, and I wanted a relationship that was real, steadfast and unwavering. A relationship I could actualize each day, seven days a week. One that could be demonstrated and integrated into my being and beliefs about life and goodness.

All dogma and indoctrination aside, I believed there were few, if any, avenues available that could help me create this spiritual relationship with God. At least until I discovered the Unity Church. Finally a church that allowed me the time and space to be with my own concept of God. Its all-encompassing, humanitarian and natural principles resonated with my spirit. I also attended the Institute for Spiritual Development, an organization that helped me develop my spirituality and confidence. I did not attend either regularly, and bounced back and forth between them. Some Sundays I didn't go to either church because I was too depressed and sullen.

Co-DA and Miracles

J didn't know where the depression came from. Perhaps from the void from not being connected to my spirit or life purpose. Or maybe I was just "coming down" from having lived in a hyper-vigilant state all of the time with my soon-to-be ex-husband. As I began to think about approaching the work for my mental and psychological health, I found out about a support group called Co-dependents Anonymous, or just Co-DA, just like the book title. I thought I could handle a small group setting and hoped it might be more enjoyable than the constant reading I was doing to heal myself.

The meeting location was only a few blocks from home, so one evening after work, I walked up past Dupont Circle and found the building. I lingered around the entrance for several minutes, hesitant to enter. Finally, I took a deep breath and went in. I pulled up a chair and joined the group warily. After listening to a few members discuss their recovery incidences, I mentally compared my situation to theirs and came to the judgment that I was at the wrong group meeting. I thought, "These people are just too odd." I had not yet recognized that they were reflecting my issues back at me.

I left before the group adjourned and, as I walked home, I thought about what I'd heard in the presentations. I was intrigued with the title, *A Course in Miracles*. One attendee had described its healing psychological power. "What a neat title," I thought.

Several weeks passed and I compulsively used my free time by going to the gym, visiting bookstores for self-help books, fixing up my apartment and going to museums. I continued to "watch my back" on the streets and live in mild fear. On Sunday mornings, I'd jog down to the Kennedy Center and sit by the harbor. At eight in the morning, it was desolate, glorious and peaceful. I sat on the pier, daydreaming about the life I wanted. Only the birdies, the gentle, lapping waves and the sun greeted me with their solace and hope for new things. I felt renewed after my talks with God, having pictured his face in the middle of the sun. I jogged back home, eager to shower and get dressed to go across town to the **YES** bookstore.

I loved that bookstore and its wonderful selection of self-help, religious, mystical, psychological and cooking books. I would spend all afternoon browsing and soaking in the knowledge from my friendly books. There were hundreds of great books that reminded me of my childhood for, even though we lived near the poverty line, we always had plenty of great books to read.

As I approached the exit with a bag of new books, I stopped to read the bulletin board crammed with business cards and notes for all kinds of activities, businesses, and events. My eyes rested on one that said: "*Course in Miracles* work group, call 202-555-5554." I thought, "What a coincidence," and was "prompted" to jot down the telephone number before hurrying home to devour my new books.

Once back in my little sanctuary, before settling down to read one of my new books titled *Prospering Woman*, I went to the bathroom and noticed that the bulbs flickered and then burned out. There was something about the light bulbs in that apartment, for I was changing bulbs every other week. They seemed to flicker and burn out more frequently than I had ever experienced. "Such a quick turn-over with light bulbs," I thought. "How strange!" (Later, I would learn that it was the intense energy in my apartment that was transitioning with me during my psychological and spiritual healing. The spiritual energy was very forceful and intense. I didn't know this at the time, and just kept the bathroom vanity stocked with extra light bulbs.)

A few days later, I called the number for the *Course in Miracles* work group. A gentle voice answered the phone, enthusiastically welcoming me to join the group. He introduced himself and provided me with the directions and time. Just before he hung up, he said, "Your life will be transformed."

The next Monday night, I exited the Metro thinking to myself that I was just going to be around some type of Bible freaks, so I'd better prepare an exit strategy in case I wanted to leave before the session ended. About seven people were gathered in a lovely renovated home near 6th and Massachusetts Avenue. It was a low pressure group in which each person shared how the "course" had changed his or her life. I was the only Black person there. The instructor described how a student needs to begin the workbook on the first day of the year, read a lesson each day, ultimately completing 365 days of individual lessons, which was supposed to change my perspective and outlook on life.

He went on to explain how the book came into existence. It was written by two spiritually grounded psychotherapists. The words in the book were "dictated" to them directly from God through channeling. It was all very mystical and I was intrigued, but not totally sold on it. I nonchalantly purchased the thick book with the very thin pages, which were light to the touch, almost like the Bible. The book sat on my mantle for weeks. I would occasionally flip through it, finding powerful phrases such as, "There is only love or fear." One day I read the statement, "The Holy Spirit will help you reinterpret everything that you perceive as fearful, and teach you only what is loving is true." (p. 74). This gentle invitation made me plop down on the sofa, awestruck. I had a strong realization that I was being called. I could no longer procrastinate.

When January 1 rolled around, I had my *Course in Miracles* book opened to Part 1, Lesson 1 on my kitchen table, as I was ready to commit to something far greater than me. As I approached Lesson 1, I struggled to understand what I was reading for it was difficult at first. The words and phrases were so foreign to me, so I kept reading over and over. I found that if I stopped struggling and just read it, then I would reflect on it during the day, and finally "get it."

The process worked! It was a slow "brain cleansing" that forced me to rid my mind of all of the longstanding fear, and embrace the Holy Spirit. When I realized I was a co-creator in my life, guided by the Holy Spirit, I felt strengthened and hopeful. I loved the new way of thinking about my life and where my power source came from. Some of my favorite passages were:

1. "The mind is very powerful, and never loses its creative force. It never sleeps. Every instant it is creating. It is hard to recognize that, thought and belief combine into a power surge that can literally move mountains." (p. 27.)
2. "There are no idle thoughts. All thinking produces form at some level." (p. 27.)
3. "Fear is really nothing and love is everything." (p. 28.)
4. "The ego is a wrong-minded attempt to perceive yourself as you wish to be, rather than as you are." (p. 37.)
5. "You have no idea of the tremendous release and deep peace that comes from meeting yourself and your brothers totally without judgment. When you recognize what you are and what your brothers are, you will realize that judging them in any way is without meaning." (p. 42.)
6. "Nothing real can be increased except by sharing. That is why God created you." (p. 64.)
7. "The communication link that God Himself placed within you, joining your mind with His, cannot be broken." (p. 250.)
8. "Be humble before Him, and yet great in Him. And value no plan of the ego before the plan of God." (p. 288.)

I did transform my life by reading one lesson a day for 365 days. Some daily lessons were more difficult than others because they asked more of me. I loved how the lessons were written; the gentle, loving guidance was addicting. I was renewed, strengthened and reunited with my Creator's spirit. I had a new framework for how I perceived events and people. I began to see the goodness in myself and in everyone around me. Fear began to remove itself from my psyche, as I was able to see the existence of Love in everything. I was no longer separated from God by my ego. Each day I began to practice my new beliefs. I had worked through a personal transformation which brought me closer to God. In glory to God, I painted a saying from the "Course" and framed it. It read:

> *"Even in the face of all Hell,*
> *I Affirm, Assert, and Decree,*
> *I am victorious in all that I do!*
> *I am Successful NOW!*
> *I attract health, wealth, and all good things of life!*
> *I am forgiving, tolerant and understanding.*
> *I love everyone!"*

I hung the framed saying on the back of my oak door, over the face of the monster. Every day, before leaving the apartment, I read the saying aloud. I was changing. My outlook was shifting radically, and I became more positive and optimistic about my life. At work, people started calling me a "Pollyanna" because I was so positive, enthusiastic and optimistic about life. I was very hopeful and began to believe the power that resided in me, my thoughts and my ways of thinking. I didn't mind being called a Pollyanna because I was starting to see the actual positive results in my life. I began to attract good things to me … and it all started with my thoughts and beliefs.

The Angel's Presence

I began to believe that I had the *grace* from God to change my life. With this faith, I began to tackle unusual and difficult activities. I wrote a nice letter to the IRS apologizing for the error and agreed upon a payment plan of $50 month to repay my debt. In three years, I would no longer be delinquent. I became very cautious about filing my annual taxes and was determined to clean up my finances.

I also decided to overcome my fear of singing in public, so I joined a Church choir. I loved singing in the choir and the choir director loved my voice, so after a few months, I was asked to sing a solo. I was nervous and unsure before my first attempt at a solo. During the first few stanzas, my voice was shaky and I started to sweat but then something happened and I began to smile. Then the nervousness just left and I started to *really* enjoy it. When the song ended, I received a wonderful applause. I was asked again and again to sing songs on Sunday and I loved preparing, practicing, and visualizing myself singing joyously on Sunday.

My solos seemed to help heal my broken spirit, and I sang *Our Father, Amazing Grace, One Voice* and *The Wind beneath My Wings*. Often, my eyes would well up with tears as I sang these lovely, soulful songs, for they seemed to bring back memories of my mother, my grandmother and how precious life is. I rocked! My favorite song to sing at the Christmas service was *O Holy Night*.

I packed the church pews because I sang from my heart. I learned how to sing loudly and strongly. I gave God "my all" when I sang. While singing *O Holy Night* one Christmas eve, I felt as if I was in "the zone" and became the notes of the song. I lost myself in the passion and gratitude I was feeling on that night. I remembered that elated feeling so well and was really happy that Christ was born to save all of us.

When I finished singing that night, a little old lady came up to me and said, "You sang so beautifully." And after a slight pause, she added, "I need to share this with you. While you were singing, I saw a huge angel standing behind you."

What a gift she had given me with her vision, and I thanked her for sharing it. As I hugged her, I said, "Yes, I did feel like I was enveloped in something or someone. Perhaps the rapture of God or one of his Archangels." I had indeed felt the presence.

To get back in touch with nature, where I believe that God finds each of us, I volunteered with the Sierra Club, which sponsored weekend outings to expose "underprivileged" children to the wonders of nature. Some of the kids were really mischievous and rowdy because no one had taught them how to honor and behave toward nature. On these nature walks and picnics, I became the teacher and the disciplinarian, using firm words but showing kindness with the kids.

The Power of Affirmations

*I*n the many books I had purchased, I kept seeing reading about the importance of affirmations during a healing process. I was slow in getting started with these. At first, developing my own affirmations was a strange process, almost humorous to me. After feeling like a victim for such a long time, I thought, "Who am I to actively create and shape what I want?" It seemed like an empty exercise … until my affirmations began to change things. I slowly saw how my beliefs through written words began to be manifested. I framed the affirmations I created in 1990, and they are still my affirmations to this day. They read:

"Every day, in every way, I am getting better and better.
Everything is coming to me easily with the Universe's timing.
I am filled with light, love, and completeness.
I am enough.
I have everything I need to enjoy my here and now.
Everything I need to know lies deep within me.
I love and appreciate myself, just as I am.
I take care of my little girl within.
The more I love myself, the more love I have to give others.
I always have a wonderful, caring, loving helpmate.

I love to love and be loved.
I am attracting to me, a wonderful, spiritual male life partner.
I give and receive freely.
This is a very rich universe and there is plenty for all of us.
I am vibrantly healthy and radiantly beautiful.
I determine my own value and beauty within and without.
The Light of God within me is producing perfect results in every phase of my life now!"

I got my courage to go back to the support group, "Co-dependents Anonymous" (CoDA). I was very attentive, more focused, and, for several months, attended each weekly meeting. I learned how to forgive myself, how to make amends for the things I regretted doing, and most importantly, I learned to accept a power greater than me to handle all of my affairs. Giving my burdens to God and releasing the control I *thought* I had was an epiphany.

I remembered an acquaintance from the CoDA group telling me she started every day with a prayer:

"Holy Spirit, help me, protect me, and direct me."

I told her how much I loved her prayer and began saying it every day before leaving for work. As I locked my apartment door, I would recite it aloud. It really made things appear differently: my days seemed to flow more smoothly, little things that used to irritate me disappeared and I always felt protected. What a gift she gave me!

The CoDA group really helped me but when I realized I was not learning anything new in the group, and when it seemed to serve as a just social circle for many, I stopped attending. I was not interested in meeting any guys or dating anyone. I left the support group on good terms, feeling enriched and awakened.

The Mean Supervisor

*A*t this time, many changes were occurring at the workplace. Our quality assurance office had been reorganized and was eventually merged into another field office operation. Some of my friends were relocated to different offices, and my special friend, Kyle, had left the organization for a better position at another federal agency. I really missed walking home from work with him, discussing people, issues and psychology. I missed his support and his intellect. His empathy and compassion enabled me to feel safely guided during my emotional and spiritual healing. He was a great teacher, and I eagerly absorbed everything he had advised. I was lonely for my friend. Feeling sentimental, I wrote:

What Is A Good Friend?

A good friend is somebody who can tease you without hurting your feelings.
A good friend tells you when your nose is runny or your hair is funny.
A good friend can make a loud fart on the elevator with you — but he warns you first.
A good friend suggests something else to do when you want to have a drink.
A good friend gently reminds you of your promises to yourself.
He listens, yells with you, laughs with you, and tells you what's on his mind.
A good friend lets you know when you're being pushy, and stands up for himself.
Sometimes he needs you more than you want him to, but that's okay. You love him.
A good friend needs his own space, just like you, but knows when he's had enough of it and finds you.
A good friend never abandons you. Even when he's not there, you still feel him with you and
you laugh at something you remembered he said.
A good friend touches you and you feel nice, because it doesn't mean anything else.
A good friend always sees the real you, not your new dress or old boots, but he'll tell you when you look strange.

A good friend sometimes gets on your last nerve; so you take a deep breath
. . . and you understand, because you love him.
He doesn't pretend, he listens, he challenges, he's there.
I'll always have a good friend.
© 1990 G. Myers

In the new office, I had a new supervisor. She was short, brown, round and bold. She also had a mean streak and for some reason I seemed to invoke her cruel side. I had become very supportive of other women, open to new ideas, optimistic and genuine. Although I had a good reputation throughout the agency, I had been a part of the quality assurance program, which had been a high visibility program, staffed with especially high-quality professionals who had received unique recognition, additional funding, and in some cases, special treatment. This situation had garnered the envy of others in the agency.

Joining this new field office operation was politically awkward for me but I knew I would adjust to the change, meet new people, and hopefully make some new friends. I quickly learned my new duties, which were responding to congressional correspondence, monitoring and evaluating field office productivity with case processing and attending a lot of meetings. I learned my tasks with minimal instruction from others. I asked questions and sought out assistance when I needed it.

My supervisor appeared to me a harsh, crude and coarse person. She had no tact in her communication with others and demonstrated very little sympathy towards them. Each day, I did my best to avoid any interaction with her. I also tried hard to not make any mistakes because she seemed to enjoy correcting my work and humiliating me at the same time. On many days, I would often leave the office feeling belittled, discouraged and humiliated.

One day I asked her, "Why are you so mean to me?" to which she replied, "Because you're such a Pollyanna. I need to make you meaner. More like me."

I was taken aback by her response and realized I'd better find another job very quickly because I did *not* want to become like her. I was trying to evolve spiritually and wanted to live in the light, not her

120

darkness. To survive this woman's cruelty, I decided to meditate for about 20 minutes every morning before going to the office. When I did this, I became more peaceful and accepting, which really helped me deflect her negative energy. I consistently meditated every single day for about a year.

At first, learning to meditate was difficult. I had so much idle chatter racing across my mind, and it took several attempts to finally arrive at a mental "clearing." I began by just taking long relaxing breaths and then just focusing on my breathing. Once I began to look at how I was breathing, the mindless chatter seemed to subside. After focusing on my breathing for about five minutes, I eventually started to feel the sensations of tingling through my veins and the "silence"; the "tingling" was my Life Force energy. I also envisioned a triangle in my mind, which helped me focus more.

To surround myself with spiritual protection, I decided to begin each meditation session with a prayer and recited the following words:

> **Surrender:** "I unconditionally surrender to you, God, all of my body, all of my mind, all of my soul, all of my affairs, and all of my freewill, so that Your Will may be done through me.
> **Dedication:** I dedicate all of myself and all of my God-given talents to the service of the Light and to the Masters and Brothers of Light to use me throughout each day and night.
> **Realization:** I thank you, God, that every person, every condition, every circumstance, every situation and everything that enters my life is always *Divinely ordered, Divinely planned, and Divinely executed* in perfect accordance with Divine Law and the will of the Father for me."
> — Lorr & Crary, p.13

With my daily meditating and raising my vibration to a higher realm, I was becoming so enlightened that I could feel her negative aura coming towards me as she approached my desk. By the time she arrived, I was able to not react to her ingenious cruelties. Through meditation, I was also able to respond to her barbs and criticisms gently and peacefully, without responding negatively.

I was constantly tested. One day, I submitted a training request form for some very interesting training I wanted to attend. I had paid in advance for this training with my own money because I really wanted to attend it for my own personal growth. It was a great National Training Laboratory (NTL) class that focused on improving interpersonal relationships, receiving feedback from others, and centering. I had mentioned this training session to my supervisor very early on in an effort to make sure I had her firm approval before spending my money. She agreed to the training without incident, so I was happy yet cautious.

In the afternoon of the day before the class, my supervisor approached me and told me how she needed me in the office that week. Even though I explained how I had the assistance of my co-workers to manage my tasks for the few days I would be away, she didn't seem to care and I left the office in tears. While walking towards home, I wondered why she enjoyed doing this to me. When I arrived at my apartment, I finished crying long and hard, and asked God to deliver me from this woman's cruelty.

Later that evening, she called me at home and told me I could attend the training. I was relieved but still *very* determined to find a way to escape from her sadism. I also made a promise to myself that if I ever became a manager, I would *never* do this to anyone. Life in the workplace is hard enough without mean managers creating petty problems. Why add to the strife? Managers may not realize how much they impact the life quality of the people who work with them and the organization's culture. My view is that employees are to be honored and embraced as a part of the workplace family.

Positive Thinking

In addition to my regular meditation, I also began reading all the books I could find about positive thinking, optimism, and creating and maintaining your own positive energy. I learned about the power of *optimism*. Optimistic thinking is learning how to interrupt your negative trains of thought, monitoring these automatic thoughts, and questioning whether your automatic thoughts are actually your *own* thoughts or learned ways of thinking. It requires analyzing how you think about things and why you maintain a certain thought pattern (p. 62, McGinnis). For example, why do people silently talk themselves out of taking mild risks in life? Is it because they have internalized a negative message about how they "will never mount to nothin'?

I began to challenge my own thinking and patterns of thought. I reflected often about the messages I had learned from adults or siblings that were no longer serving a purpose for me. I began to be more mindful of any limiting beliefs and thoughts I had automatically absorbed, and began to replace those with positive affirmations. I wanted to reshape my life from the inside out, so I started with my own pattern of thinking.

I would often go for long walks after work. I'd walk through downtown Washington, D.C., viewing the monuments, the Capitol, the White House, the Lincoln Memorial and the Jefferson Memorial, and think about my life purpose and what I wanted to become. I reflected about the mistakes and poor judgment I'd made, the lost time, and why I made the decisions I made. I watched the wealthy at the valet parking spots, eager to take in another theatrical spectacle. I wondered what it might be like to be in their shoes. Were they really happy or just image-laden with the accouterments of success? I wondered what success would look like for me. What did I want out of life?

Asking for Help

$\mathcal{E}$ach day, I could feel myself getting stronger, but there were the little missteps that asked me to look more closely at my healing process. When I watched romantic movies, I observed the lovers in the movie with disgust. When I watched poignant movies known as "tear jerkers," I was incapable of shedding tears. There was a hard edge in my being that had helped me cope with survival, yet at the same time, this callousness prevented me from displaying any delicate emotions. I was removed and distant from the precious sentiments of life. My romantic feelings and natural "gushiness" had left.

The only feelings that seemed to surface were in the nightmares I endured regularly. I had recurring dreams about Doug's face, in which I would always dream about running from him, only to be slowed down in the muddy road that allowed him to catch up to me. I dreamed about his scowl, his evil eyes and his threats. Finally, I would awaken to see the soft surroundings of my new home, but drenched with sweat and in fear. I wondered when the nightmares would stop. Why did I keep seeing movies about domestic abuse? When would I be okay?

I realized I might need some help to work through the issues that kept me from relaxing and feeling at peace. Whenever driving around the area, I would always avoid the Silver Spring where I had once lived because I had flashbacks of the torture and pain. My body would react to the old memories with alarm and panic. I needed to talk with someone who could help me forget about my past. But who?

Even though I was making great progress with my spiritual healing, there were some thoughts I had that would not go away. My subconscious seemed to be rife with danger and fear. My cells seemed to have remembered the pain and travesty of a relationship gone bad. A deeper healing was needed that I was incapable of discovering for myself.

In defiance of my self-sufficiency, my Black culture, and my independence, I sought therapeutic help. Fortunately, my health plan provided for 8 weeks of counseling and therapy. While completing the application for psychological therapy, I reminisced about the first time I had sought counseling assistance, and I wondered why Doug couldn't enter counseling and therapy to heal himself? Why couldn't we have worked on this together? Why was therapy ostracized and viewed so negatively by him? Was it a Black man thing?

I wished that all of the macho crap would melt in the Black culture. I knew of so many Black men who needed psychological help but their massive egos prevented them from seeking it. Instead, they turned to physically abusing women, frequent violence, unprotected sex and drugs to escape looking at who and what they were. Instead of blaming "the man," they needed to look in the mirror and see the comfortable victim they had conveniently created. They have so much potential and strength that is suffocated by their exaggerated machinations about a legendary enemy.

I know life is a struggle and unfair. It ain't easy. But when I see so many gifted, beautiful, strong Black men taking the easier, painless route, I am disgusted and ashamed. They seemed to have forgotten about what is possible and how they themselves reflect the image of God.

In examining how I could further improve, I discovered this statement about emotional wellness. It states:

Eight Traits of Emotional Wellness
The key to our emotional wellness, researchers believe,
Rests in possessing the following eight traits:
The ability to step back and look at yourself honestly;
The ability to change;
The ability to increase your boundaries of responsibility;
The ability to take responsibility for your own thoughts, feelings,
and actions;
The ability to trust and be open to your feelings;
The ability to tolerate stress;
The ability to be flexible;
The ability to recognize when you have a problem.
(Author unknown)

I could clearly see I had a problem. I was repulsed regularly by displays of intimacy, trust and any type of romance. Displays of affection and tenderness were foreign to me. I was still having nightmares and anxiety attacks about close, upfront contact with men, and I knew something was wrong. I had a problem and needed help.

I Need Therapy

After completing the intake form at the counseling office, I scheduled an appointment for the following week. The counselor assigned to me had a similar name like my own, which was very comforting to me in a strange way. I thought maybe she would show some additional empathy towards me?

I predicted that during the counseling sessions, I would have to talk about uncomfortable subjects and that my defensive boundaries would be slowly chiseled away so that the "real me" would be exposed. I was afraid of, once again, telling my life details and current idiosyncrasies to a complete stranger. After all, I thought I was making great progress on my own. Would I be proven wrong again? Would she tell me I was beyond repair, damaged goods and truly a crazy person?

Her sessions were gentle and probing. As I walked home from each one, I thought deeply about what we had discussed. I began to see myself in a more hopeful light, understanding my own decisions, needs, desires and environment. Many sorrowful buried incidents surfaced during the counseling sessions. I became more aware of my life events and occurrences, and began to understand how I was affected by them. I was no longer blaming myself all the time. I began to understand and see how I was very similar to other people and how they made their choices for survival.

Being involved in therapy and getting really authentically involved is a very raw and intense process during which ideas, thoughts and strong feelings come up to the surface without your permission. I could be in the grocery store selecting apples and immediately become sad and start to cry because the apples would remind me of a sad incident. Once, I was leaving a movie theatre with a good girl friend, having just watched the movie *Thelma and Louise*, and began to cry uncontrollably right on the sidewalk. The themes in that movie of rape, violence, justice and suicide really echoed within me, and the emotions just poured out. Thank goodness I had a wonderful, supportive friend with me who understood what I was going through.

Even though the therapy and counseling process are intense, the benefits outweigh the arduous process. You learn to uncover hidden messages and behavioral routines that prevent a fulfilling life. I think a lot of people need therapy to overcome destructive, problematic behaviors and illnesses, such as verbal and physical abuse, alcoholism, eating disorders, shopping and gambling addictions, work, relationship and sexual addictions, and depression.

Unfortunately, comparatively few individuals acknowledge they have a problem and seek out therapy due to the stigma associated with "getting therapy" or "seeing a shrink" in our society. Sadly, as sophisticated as we are in war technologies and the promotion of pharmaceuticals, we still have not addressed the fundamental core and source of the ills in our society. And we still place mental illness on the lowest rung of our ladder of acceptance.

Our world would be better if each of us started to look within ourselves, before placing any blame on others. Just think about it. Organization life would be healthier with fewer or no petty political games or cruelties. People would be cared for and cared about, instead of being on the receiving end of sarcasm, jokes and thoughtlessness. I have a favorite saying that reminds me to look with myself first, to correct my own actions before pointing to others. It reads:

"You can become master if you will first master yourself.
Instead of trying first to correct others, look at yourself
And realize what you are thinking, speaking, feeling, and acting.
Then assert self-discipline and build towards self-mastery!"

— R. Crary

My Therapy Process

Therapy was all about looking within, inside the self. I looked at my addictions and compulsive behaviors, and I claimed my ownership for my life choices. I no longer chose to be the victim in my life, blaming others for my situation. I wanted to take charge and get on with it!

My therapy process seemed to follow the pattern of talking with the therapist, spending time reflecting on the conversation later, and then having spontaneous "Ah ha" moments! Each week I would visit the psychologist to answer her probing questions, and would talk and talk and talk, so the allotted 50 minutes would fly by.

After leaving the office and walking home, I'd think about the conversation. Sometimes I would have clearer insights about past events and sometimes I'd be even more confused. On many occasions, I'd just be sad from wishing I could have fixed things when they'd happened, or said different words to someone, or had been more assertive or courageous. I felt as though I had just let things happen to me while I was growing up. I didn't make waves, but had tried hard to cooperate and to be Daddy's obedient little girl.

Can I Undo the Past, Please?

I often wondered why I couldn't stop my parents' fighting. Why couldn't I have protected my brothers better? Why didn't I stand up to Dad when he was being mean and obnoxious? I finally learned from my therapy and counseling sessions that I had done the best I could have done at that time, as a child, as a teenager and as a young woman. It happened that way due to my tiny level of awareness at the time, and due to my own desire for approval and acceptance. I was painfully unaware of my circumstance and plight at the time.

I learned I couldn't undo the past. I could only honor it and learn from it, by not repeating the same mistakes. I came to believe everything happens to us for a reason, so that we can evolve and learn from it. I endured life's hardships only to make me stronger, wiser, and more compassionate. I had to either change or stay stuck in playing a victim's role. I chose to change.

Awareness

While wanting to change, I became more alert about my patterns of thinking and my behaviors. I examined and became more aware of the forces that had shaped me and my decisions. Awareness is everything! Without awareness and being fully present "in the moment," life ends up being a patchwork of delayed reactions to situations. It's the feeling that you can never catch up to a train that's just left the station. No matter how fast you run, you're always going to be late.

How did I end up in an abusive relationship? Because I was unaware of how I had internalized and interpreted actions, events and messages in my early environment. I had been extremely impressionable and sensitive to my surroundings, so I had absorbed all the messages, behavior patterns and ways of coping that seemed to serve me well at that chaotic time.

These messages, ideas and behaviors I had internalized from an early childhood meshed nicely with a controlling and abusive man. My own low self-esteem, co-dependent nature and willingness to be second class to a man made the two of us fit like hand and glove. I am not a psychologist, but I've learned how the human mind amazingly adjusts to help a person survive all kinds of trauma, hardships and subtle cruelties. This coping mechanism serves us well until it's no longer needed in new and different situations.

Unfortunately, some people keep up the same coping methods that are no longer suitable for the new situation they find themselves in, and then wonder why things aren't working better for them. They don't receive counseling or therapy to explore their compulsive behaviors or obsessions. Simply put, my therapy helped me explore these past messages and coping behaviors, and I learned how to mentally readjust for a better life, ultimately attracting new situations to me. I eventually learned that we attract to ourselves what we hold in our minds.

The Daily Work

Throughout therapy, I learned how to be more aware of my choices, how I rationalized events, and how I had learned negative messages. I began to see that I could start to re-shape these processes to become a healthier person with a more rewarding life.

I still visited bookstores and sought out workbooks that would help me practice and improve my thought patterns on a daily basis. First, I had to tackle and "un-do" the negative messages I had internalized as a child, the distorted, catastrophic thinking (anxiety), the old belief system that no longer served me, and my dysfunctional thought patterns.

Before erasing the negative messages, I had to be fully aware of all of them. It had taken years to internalize all of the negative messages, so I knew it would be a gradual, daily process of being mindful to acknowledge them whenever they surfaced. But it could take years to replace them with positive, affirming messages.

For all of us, these negative messages come from long-held beliefs about ourselves that we have taken for granted and assumed were real. For example, some women have learned: "It isn't lady-like to show anger," or, have internalized the belief: "Life is a struggle," or that, "All women should be skinny." These negative messages come from deeper underlying beliefs learned from parents, teachers, our peers and even society, and do not serve our purpose for a healthy, fulfilling life. I had to decide which new messages would support a healthy and prosperous life for me, and which to toss out.

To overcome these negative beliefs, which often caused much anxiety and worry, I began to replace the negative beliefs with positive mental "self-talk." Instead of thinking: "I'll never get a promotion," I began saying to myself, "My perfect job is right around the corner." To improve my beliefs about my physical appearance, when I looked into the mirror, I told myself, "Gina, you're gorgeous."

Me gorgeous? That one was really a big leap. It was very strange and awkward for me to look into my own eyes and exclaim what a lovely, perfect person I was. What helped me achieve *believing* in this positive message was thinking about how much God loves me and how He doesn't make mistakes. I began to recognize how I shined in God's eyes. I also discovered a wonderful piece by Marianne Williamson, that reads:

> *"Our deepest fear is not that we are inadequate. Our deepest fear is that we are powerful beyond measure. It is our light not our darkness that most frightens us. We ask ourselves who am I to be brilliant, gorgeous, talented and fabulous. Actually, who are you not to be? You are a child of God. Your playing small doesn't serve the world. There is nothing enlightened about shrinking so that other people won't feel insecure around you!*
>
> *We are born to manifest the glory of God that is within us. It's not just in some of us; it's in everyone, and as we let our own light shine, we consciously give other people permission to do the same. As we are liberated from our own fear, our presence automatically liberates others."*

These words awakened my soul. They called out to me and said, "Live it!" To keep the words in my psyche, I had an artist frame a wonderful color photograph of Nelson Mandela with Marianne's magical words underneath it. It hangs in my office and serves as a reminder to me of my own greatness.

I found it important to post pictures, affirmations, sayings and anything else that would help me focus my mind on possibilities and prosperity. Positive words and statements had to fully saturate my existence to repair the damage of the past. (I recommend a really superb workbook to help with these positive messages, and any anxieties. Titled, *The Anxiety and Phobia Workbook* by Edmund J. Bourne, Ph.D., it's really an excellent workbook, with wonderful exercises and advice, and is very clearly written.)

From this workbook, I also learned how to manage my fears and eventually destroy them by realizing that they were caused by my distorted thinking. For example, I often feared meeting new people, believing they would judge me in a negative light, as my ex-husband had done. When I started to think about how it had never happened with new people, I began to do "self-talk" to reflect on my success in these types of situations. On page 187 in the workbook, Bourne discusses three different types of distortions:

1. Overestimating a negative outcome (i.e., exaggerating the worse case scenario).
2. Catastrophizing (e.g., "I'll never live it down," or, "They'll never forgive me."
3. Underestimating your ability to cope (e.g., "If something bad happens, I won't be able to handle it!").

Bourne defines "fear" as: *the unreasonable overestimation of some threat, coupled with an underestimation of your ability to cope.*

I was often caught up with overestimating a negative outcome or underestimating my ability to cope, and I really used this workbook to sort out my thinking patterns. After following the exercises in the workbook over many months and maintaining my daily awareness of my thought patterns, I slowly began to feel more confident about my life and my possibilities. I restated again and again, my favorite affirmation:

Gina Myers

> *"In the face of all Hell,*
> *Affirm, Assert and Decree!*
> *I am successful now!*
> *I am forgiving, tolerant, and understanding and*
> *I love everyone."*
>
> — *A Course In Miracles*

Boundary Management

A big part of my healing process was being able to determine what was right for me in terms of my own beliefs, thoughts, values and ideas. How did I manage the information and ideas I encountered from others? I became more aware during conversations with others of how people can say some things and unwittingly crush your outlook. I was able to see how we all regularly make casual statements that denigrate ourselves and others. Without thinking, we say things like, "You're so stupid!" or "You'll never get that right," or, "You can't hang?" or, "Who do you think you are?"

It took effort to maintain positive self-talk and a healthy outlook. I began to understand I would have to actively and assertively manage what I absorbed and what I rejected. I learned about *boundary management*, which was managing my own boundaries. It was about thinking for myself instead of agreeing with and always trying to please others. Selecting and choosing what I wanted to absorb from others, and what I would not tolerate from others.

Codependent people have a boundary issue. We are so busy fulfilling the needs of other people that we often forget where we begin and the other person ends. We plan, anticipate, and even feel for the other person more than ourselves. We do not manage our boundaries in a healthy manner for a variety of reasons. There needs to be a good *balance* with how we accept, absorb and reject outside stimuli. If we reject everything, we don't learn or adapt to new situations. If we accept everything, we erode who we are, and lose our intrinsic selves.

"Boundaries should be distinct enough to preserve our individuality, yet open enough to admit new ideas and perspectives. They should be firm enough to keep our values and priorities clear, open enough to communicate our priorities to the right people, yet closed enough to withstand assault from the thoughtless and the mean."

— *Boundaries: Where You End and I Begin,* p.81.

I learned how to manage my boundaries. I had stopped anticipating, thinking and planning for others and begun to enjoy the freedom of just thinking about me—my wants, needs and desires. I no longer had to "second guess" someone else's thoughts for my own safety. As I evolved through this boundary management process, I eventually discovered that: "I am an important and valuable person who is capable in all situations and deserving of the respect and attention of those who are important to me in my life!"

This statement became a new affirmation for me, which I posted on my refrigerator door.

Expressions

During my healing process, I found ways to artistically express what I was feeling and emoting. I painted with water colors, wrote poetry, journaled to record my insights, did gourmet cooking and visited Mother Nature often. I was on a rollercoaster ride of emotions. I was depressed at times, began to grieve my Mother's death, and began to work through my anger towards men. I still had frequent nightmares about the abuse and the stalking, even though they had apparently stopped.

My artistic side had been repressed for many years, so when I impulsively purchased a water color set, I was amazed at the art I could create. The process seemed to allow my soul to communicate with me. I painted lots of flowers and nature settings plus some strange pictures that helped me release my pent-up longings. There was something peaceful about the wet brush gliding across the paper, exuding its soft colors. Painting was a form of meditating.

I also wrote in my journal often. I rarely knew how I filled the pages; I just began to write and the words came. During my grieving process, I was filled with rage and bitterness over my mother's "departure" and wrote:

> *I think of the past and become sad as I remember the full and*
> *beautiful happy moments*
> *Only to be relived through different eyes.*
> *Eyes that feel the warmth dissipating through a hardened*
> *perspective, becoming more aware, sophisticated, and*
> *less sensitive.*
> *My family has changed.*
> *We are no longer united.*
> *We have become enemies, no longer with common dreams, but*
> *separated hopes, and ambitions.*
> *All because of an expired and dead spirit of a woman.*
> *A woman who once had the power and the magic to hold, mold, and*
> *unite.*
> *I will never forgive you for instilling false promises and images of a*
> *life that you knew nothing of.*
> *I will never forgive you for dying, for leaving us, groping in the*
> *darkness for a flame of ideals.*
> *Only to be burned by a sick, but truthful reality.*
> © 1990 Gina Myers

My emotions were raw and piercing. Whenever I saw babies on television or held a baby, I was woefully reminded of what I had done. I began to grieve the abortions I'd had, and I regretted being the one to tell those young spirits in my womb that it wasn't their time yet; only because I didn't want them. They were an inconvenience in my life at that time. I know that murder is a sin and I ask to be forgiven. I pondered which was more painful—a chaotic and dangerous life or an early death? It was a choice I made.

Each woman has to make her own choice because each situation is different. For those who are strongly opposed to abortion and a woman's right to choose, please stand in line at city adoption centers and register your name and address, and commit to raising the newborns who might live in dangerous and poor conditions. Right now, there are many babies of all races and ethnicities who need good, warm, loving homes right here in the United States. So sign up!

I also wrote about my evolving depression and pondered its source. I thought that perhaps my brain chemistry had shifted after the constant hyper-vigilance and non-stop adrenaline surges from my "fight or flight" mode during the domestic violence periods. I never really knew when the depression was planning a visit. I just found myself feeling sad and hopeless, wondering why everything seemed so bleak. When I first started having these "low moments," I speculated that it was probably just a hormonal, menstrual thing that would eventually fade away. But the dark moods became longer, deeper and bleaker. As I began to journal the episodes, I realized it was seasonal. There was a specific time period, like clockwork, with the onset of winter. Deep winter seemed to prolong my despair, with the depression arriving every November. In my journal, I wrote:

November Depression

Here it comes.
It approaches me like an old friend slowly comin' down a dark alley.
Calling my name to come closer, closer, closer to
the lavender despair,
that smells of sweet smoke and the past.
Stale, strong, and silent, watching me decide
Life or death,
Love or sadness,
Strength or fear.
Making me choose.
© 1991 Gina Myers

When I started talking to my Dad again, I shared my information with him. He described how he had suffered through some similar situations. He also enlightened me about how his mother had suffered from depression every November. We talked about solutions such as medications, special lighting, nature walks, exercising, and staying busy. He also told me about *The Depression Workbook* by Copeland which had helped him a lot.

It felt good talking to him again, and I appreciated our warm chats. I was glad I had discovered the nature and context of this new enemy called depression, and he mailed his copy of the workbook to me. I read it immediately, bought my own copy, and began to work through a lot of the exercises. It helped me tremendously, and I also planned a new project to work on every November.

I often felt that part of the source of my depression was my feeling of being disconnected from God and not being in tune with my Divine mission. Depression forced me to question my life, my Higher Power and the purpose and meaning of my life. I gained a lot from those dark days. My depression made me search and question my existence. Without those dark, dangerous days, I wouldn't have the appreciation I have for the simple things in life, such as a brilliant sun, the face of a cat and the laughter of children.

After thinking about my Divine mission, I learned that my natural exuberance seemed to surface whenever I was focused on creative and beneficial endeavors for others. When I was helping others or volunteering at an organization, I would always feel great. Maybe I was learning more about my soul's journey, and perhaps depression helped me to communicate with my deepest soul, with my God-self.

I also knew that depression was caused by low levels of serotonin. I preferred to rely less on pharmaceuticals and more on natural remedies, such as more sunlight, regular exercise, a low-carb diet, positive thinking, positive people and pets. I was also fortunate that my depression was not chronic.

I continued to find ways to express my passion and to re-channel my anger. I managed to focus on new projects and hobbies, such as bicycling, hiking in the mountains, taking classes, enjoying fireworks, playing in puddles, enjoying the beach and acting silly. I was working hard to get back into life. I had missed a lot!

I continued to start out each day with a silent prayer and the reading of my *Daily Word*. I began to express my gratitude to God for helping me change my life. I started to feel buttressed by my renewed faith and devotion. Whenever I sat down to meditate, I would begin with my silent prayer and allow the stillness to enter. As I felt my closeness with God, I had often cried tears of joy and gratitude, as I enjoyed the power of this oneness. To show my gratitude, I was going to continue to develop myself and contribute great things. I made a promise to God:

"What we are is our gift from God, but what we become is our gift to God."

Finding Me!

By this time, I was in my late thirties and was beginning to feel confident, sexy and invincible! The two-year saga with the house had finally come to an end. It was sold and any profit that remained was used to pay the overdue mortgage notes. It was a huge blemish on my credit report, but my spirits were buoyed when I received my final divorce papers in the mail a few months later.

Having the drama of the divorce, the selling of the house and the violence behind me, I felt like a new woman. I had the excitement of a person who's been given another chance at life and I was going to make the most of it. I was determined to be in the game of life, and not sit on the sidelines. I was determined to become my own hero, with a fulfilling life, conquering any obstacles that came my way. Even though I continued to watch my back due to my ex-husband's stalking, I was ready to confront and conquer all of my fears.

Often I would go for a nice long stroll after work, just to free my mind of the high drama I had endured over the years. I would walk and walk, processing ideas and goals in my mind. Walking was a form of therapy for me in which I could reflect about the day I'd just had at work, and then other times, I would just daydream about my future. Walking around the city was also my show of defiance toward my ex-husband and I mentally dared him to approach me. I was ready for him this time, and felt free and invincible.

Each evening, after walking or working out at the gym, I would run a hot bath, pour in my favorite foaming bubbles, and read a self-improvement book. I wanted to reshape my attitude about life and develop my spiritual, emotional, and personal power. My favorite books to read during that time were *Dare to Be Yourself* by Cohen, *Mastery* by Leonard, *The Power of Optimism* by McGinnis, *Lucid Dreaming* by LaBerge and *Awakening: A Daily Guide to Conscious Living* by Gawain; plus all of the other books by Shakti Gawain which focused on awareness, personal power, and spiritual growth. I had an insatiable appetite for self-improvement books.

For the next several years, I followed this unique journey of self-discovery and healing. My career was going great! I had left the organization with the mean supervisor and had finally obtained a position as an organization development specialist, due to all of my experiences with organizational change. As I read voraciously and learned about my new role in the organization, I was also able to further my own personal development.

The main underpinnings of organization development are human development, organization psychology, and adult learning. I tried to practice what I was preaching! When I stood in front of a group, I could validate the theory with the actual experience. I practiced authenticity, honest communication, courage, and continual learning. Although I was striving to be a good person, I continued to disregard some of God's commandments because I exerted much effort to have fun and experience life, trying to make up for lost time.

I found so much joy doing my organizational work that I would often tell others "I'm doing the Lord's work." I really believed I was making a huge contribution by helping others in the workplace. I was fully committed to the fact that, without good working relationships and strong teams, nothing of high quality can be produced. I learned about my Myers-Briggs Type Indicator (MBTI), a personal survey that helped me realize that as an ENFP, I loved to help people achieve happiness and their true potential.

I had passion about my work, and each morning I eagerly dressed to rush off to the office for another exciting and intense day. I truly believed that I was in "dharma," that is, that my body, mind, and spirit were synchronized as I went about this wonderful, healing work. As I worked to heal others, I was healing myself. It was a great example of the cycle of giving and receiving.

To Be or Not to Be With Men

To conquer my fear of intimacy with men, I slowly began to date again. But this time, it was different. I observed more, stayed more mindful and was much more assertive. I dated men on my terms. I placed myself first and began to view men as my equal, in some things. In other things, I was far better than them, such as in multitasking, confronting and communicating. I was wholeheartedly committed to honoring myself, sometimes at the expense of others due to my still-hardened perspective about love and relationships.

With my strong apprehension about being powerless in relationships, I compartmentalized my friendships with men. I had a different buddy for different activities, and chose to keep deep intimacy out of the relationships. I knew I wasn't quite ready for an involved, deeply committed relationship with a man, for I still didn't trust them. In fact, I wasn't quite sure of how I wanted to fit them into my life, if at all. They were peripheral at the time, and I saw them as fun, amusing creatures who were not allowed to get close to my heart. Ever.

My favorite song at that time was Tina Turner's *What's Love Got to Do With It?* I liked that song because it was all about sexual passion without love. There was *no attachment*. She was my idol because she had survived an abusive relationship, as described in her book, *I Tina*. She was #1 on the charts with that song. Her passionate outlook on life resonated with mine, and I would drive down the highway, riding high in my Chevy Blazer, screaming out her songs as the radio blared. I was glad to be me; I loved life, and I thought all men were stupid jerks who allowed their little heads to guide them!

A big step for me was learning how to enjoy my own company, even if it meant going home on a Friday night without having a date for the evening. I read a lot, chose to eat alone at restaurants, rented mountain cabins on holiday weekends, took vacation trips and enjoyed nature. I enjoyed my freedom, independence and solitude for a long time.

The Gift of Solitude

During my quiet times, I was mentally processing new information. After dates, I would sit back and take the time to reflect on my behaviors, his behaviors, and explore whether my needs were being met. I was careful not to repeat the same old behaviors. I reflected and analyzed situations whenever I would start to feel a little uncomfortable with someone. The silent reflection helped me assess my intentions, provided the time to absorb my affirmations, and helped me integrate my new values and beliefs.

I acknowledged I had choices to make and actions to take. I stopped letting events happen to me, and started to shape the events. I continued my positive self-talk and often acted on my insights by "course-correcting" as necessary. I stayed fully conscious of my behaviors and circumstances, knowing I was responsible for my own quality of life.

I made a list of the things I liked to do, whether it was taking a hot bubble bath, enjoying a fine wine or hugging a tree. I explored my pleasures, indulged in ethnic cuisines, bought gifts for myself, kept fresh flowers in my apartment, and focused on my health. I began to watch a lot of movies that helped me get back in touch with my delicate emotions and tenderness. It was a great moment for me when I found myself crying at the end of a movie titled *Fluke*. I didn't watch many sensitive, romantic movies, but I watched *The Shining* starring Jack Nicholson quite frequently because I received much satisfaction and enjoyment from the ending, when the crazy husband was found frozen in the snow the next morning. That was my favorite movie for many years.

I worked on creating my own healthy image. I improved my posture, my skin, my wardrobe and continued to glorify my African and Indian hair. I became fully aware of how magazines and television commercials subtly dictated to women how they should look, feel and wear. I started shaping this for myself, ignoring these destructive messages. I wanted to look good in my clothes, to be fit and feel healthy. I was sexiest when I felt fit. Women need to focus on their health, not the boney images promoted in the media. (I really love the new Dove soap commercials. Finally, all of us are being recognized for our beautiful uniqueness, regardless of our race, ethnicity or age. Thank you, Dove soap company!)

Even now, I'm aware that honoring myself and continuing with self-exploration never ends. Each day brings a new opportunity to care for myself, before I attempt to care for others. I take the time out for *me*, when I need to. I have no problem saying "No" to a request for a favor if it feels burdensome or unreasonable. I have the luxury of living alone and I continue to enjoy it. When I start to feel my aloneness, I think about God. When I want some companionship, I call upon a friend. Life is good.

The Spiritual Journey

The Lord Heals the Brokenhearted and Binds up Their Wounds.
— *Psalm 147:3*

It's been about seventeen years since my divorce. I have strengthened my faith in God and I have learned I must obey God, following *all* the commandments. Faith in God and obedience to Him are inseparable. Each day, I remember to put God first. No matter what I have to deal with at work or at home, I open each morning with a focus on God. When I accidentally miss a morning, I feel unanchored and vulnerable. I often stop and say a silent prayer. I consistently read my *Daily Word* each morning and say my prayer to the Holy Spirit as I start up my car engine, preparing to drive to work through the Washington, D.C. traffic.

Although I know each day may have its surprises or set-backs, I feel prepared and protected by God, the Holy Spirit and my Angels. I pray often throughout the day, especially when I have a new task or encounter, or an obstacle to overcome. I say a silent prayer as I summon my courage to face the challenge. I have fully and totally surrendered to a Power greater than me. I know who really runs the show and it ain't me. Prayer changes things; it heals, strengthens and focuses. It connects us all to our Divine Power and to the Universe's love. It's my direct channel to God, and I know I would not be where I am today without Him.

I enjoy saying prayers and I enjoy finding new ones. One of my favorite prayers is Saint Theresa's Prayer:

"May today there be peace within.
May you trust God that you are exactly where you are meant to be.
May you not forget the infinite possibilities that are born of Faith.
May you use those gifts that you have received,
and pass on the love that has been given you.
May you be content knowing you are a child of God.
Let this presence settle into your bones,
And allow your soul the freedom to sing, dance, praise and love.
It is there for each and every one of us!

I also have a favorite prayer for animals:

A Prayer for Animals
"Hear our humble prayer, O God, for our friends the animals,
Especially animals who are suffering;
For any that are hunted or lost or deserted or frightened or hungry;
For all that must be put to death.
We entreat for them all Thy mercy and pity,
and for those who deal with them,
We ask a heart of compassion and gentle hands and kindly words.
Make us, ourselves, to be true friends to animals and so,
to share the blessings of the merciful."

— *Albert Schweitzer*

Through my focus on God, I have also learned about the power of positive thinking. I believe that with God, all things are possible. A positive attitude is everything. Just think about it. We attract to ourselves what we hold in our minds. If you think you can't do something, then you probably can't. If you are anticipating catching the flu during flu season, then you will. If you feel you will never get out of debt, then you won't. We have got to believe in positive outcomes, since we, ourselves are creators in our own right.

It all begins with our thoughts, and we can change things with our thoughts. I encourage everyone to read the book *Creating Affluence* by Deepak Chopra. (Pay special attention to Chapter 1.) Read it often and let each of the cells in your body absorb it. I read this book frequently and keep it next to my *Daily Word* and my *Bible*. While I drink my coffee or tea in the morning, I select readings from one of the alphabet sections. My life has changed since I have begun to focus my thoughts on positive possibilities born of faith. And I'm more prosperous.

Prosperity

"The Lord Has Prosperity to Give and Those Who Are Determined, Go After Their Share!"
— C. Fillmore, 1994

I wholeheartedly subscribe to the Laws of Prosperity. I first got an idea of what prosperity was all about from my friends Don and Kevin. Whenever I'd leave their lovely house after a visit, they would hug me and say, "Peace and Prosperity to you!" It felt like my own personal blessing, and I would drive home feeling warm and nurtured. I wanted to learn more about the keys to prosperity because the concept really intrigued me.

One afternoon in 1999, I was glancing through an adult learning catalog and saw an advertisement for a Prosperity class. It was in the evenings from 7 to 9 pm. I registered for the class and about six weeks later, I was sitting in the front row, eager to absorb the teacher's instruction. It was one of the most powerful classes I have ever taken.

It taught me how to trust God and the Universe to supply all of my needs as I continued to work hard. I learned that we build a prosperity consciousness as we base our mental creativity and thoughts on a foundation of faith. We must continually think "God thoughts," and fully overcome our thoughts of fear and lack. We must also be conscious of the words we speak that can limit our prosperity. I have a chart below that provides some examples for you. It's adapted from some of the class materials provided by P. Hinshaw.

The Power of Language

Instead of:	Use:
I can't afford it.	I prefer to buy it later, or I'll buy something else.
I'll never have enough money for that.	When I am ready for it, it will manifest.
My bank account is always a mess.	I have plenty to share and plenty to spare.
Those people get way too much for what they do.	Each person receives according to his consciousness.
Give me a break!	Let me "chill"/relax for a minute.
I can't stand it!	I will get through this.
There's never enough to go around.	There is plenty for all of us.
I'm sorry.	I feel for you or I apologize.
You're so crazy!	You're creative and talented!

The real power of the class was demonstrated in the final exercise. Each of us was instructed to bring our most prized, sentimental possession to class and be prepared to give it away to a complete stranger. The more we cared about our possession, the stronger the outcome of the exercise. For example, some people brought an item they liked but not a prized possession. Others were really into it and brought really valuable things to give away.

The purpose of the exercise was to lessen our detachment to material things and focus more on God. We were demonstrating our faith in God by letting go of something we really loved, knowing we could never really lose it in a spiritual sense. By doing this, we would be demonstrating that our needs would always be taken care of by God. I really wanted to show my belief in the Lord's prosperity, so I devoted my Raggedy Ann doll to the exercise. She was my most valued possession, for I had owned her for 35 years! I really, really loved her.

Before taking "Annie" to class, I cleaned her up and took a photo of her. My heart started to ache from having to part with her but I held back my tears. For a moment, I was going to change my mind but then thought about how cowardly that would have been. I really wanted to demonstrate my faith. I believed in prosperity and that my Higher Power, God, was taking good care of me.

In the class, we were led to the park to choose the stranger to whom we would give our possession, and I searched the faces of those there. I didn't want to give my doll to just any old person, and chose an attractive, professional-looking Black woman with sensitive eyes, who looked to be in her mid-thirties. I approached her and gave her my Raggedy Ann doll. I told her about the class we were in and why I was giving her my precious doll. I started to choke up a little, fighting back my pain. The woman was kind, open and accepting. She told me, "I'll take good care of your Raggedy Annie doll. Don't worry about her." I was so happy to hear her say that and to discover I had selected someone with a good soul.

During the remainder of the class, I was missing my doll and grew quiet. I looked at the teacher with a bit of resentment. I had stepped out of my comfort zone of fear, control, attachment and scarcity, and had walked out into a territory that was incomprehensible and foreign to me. What had I just done? I had given up something else after I'd already lost so much through the divorce.

Annie was all of my warm memories and friendships rolled into softly stuffed and painted cloth. She was so much a part of me and I had really identified with her. In fact, she had been just like me—a raggedy doll who needed protection and nurturing. I envisioned that giving away Raggedy Annie was also about letting go of a raggedy image of me. It was about time.

Since that class, I have not had any money problems. I believed there is plenty for all of us and continue to thank God for my job, my warm home, my health, my pets and a car that runs dependably. I have discovered I am very competent with money, can afford what I want, and I give and receive money and materials frequently. I do not jeopardize my success by thoughts of being unworthy; I pursue it and embrace it! Most importantly, I have learned that prosperity comes through different channels, which must be kept open by thinking, believing, creating and seizing opportunities, which all originate from God's Divine Plan. There is no limit to what is possible with God. With God, all things are possible, and I am open to all of these possibilities.

Guardian Angels

God sent Helpers my way. In fact, I think at certain times, He had all of his troops focused on me. I've had so many "close calls" and flirtations with death that I truly believe I was guided and guarded by my guardian angels. There were moments during the physical abuse episodes when I received warnings. Sometimes I was guided to leave the house just in time. Other times, while I was asleep, I'd be awakened by a shift in energy, beckoning me to get up out of the bed and to go to another room.

More recently, about eight or nine years ago, I was driving home in my Blazer on a major highway (495), with a tank full of gas and going at about 65 miles an hour. With both hands on the steering wheel, I noticed I no longer had control of the steering. The steering wheel had simply stopped working, just spinning uselessly. I realized if I were to brake, I'd be rear-ended by the speeding cars behind me. I didn't know what to do, so I just said, "Oh God!"

While still moving at 65 miles per hour, I felt the car being guided over to the side of the road and onto the shoulder! I then braked and came to a complete and safe stop. I sat still for a few moments, stunned and thinking about what had just occurred. I knew it was the action of my Guardian Angels who had been sent by God to help me. I thanked God and my Angels out loud. After a few minutes, a roadside assistance patroller drove up and I explained what had just happened with my steering wheel. Hours later, with the steering fixed, I rounded the corner toward my street, still thinking about what had just happened with the Angels.

Another time, I was driving up to Ohio on a Friday night to visit my brothers, and I got lost on Highway 68. My map was outdated and didn't reflect the new highway route. It was very dark and the road was hilly, winding and unpredictable. I'd just finished a very stressful day and was filled with nervous tension. There were no gas stations, stores or houses for many miles, and I started to cry like a baby. I said, "God, please help me. I'm so lost. Please show me something to help me get back to the main road."

I kept driving along the road, afraid to pull over on to the darkened shoulder, and suddenly, a car appeared out of nowhere with a Pennsylvania license plate. Since I was born in Pennsylvania, I said, "That's a good enough sign for me!" and began to follow the car. I followed that car for about thirty miles and was led back to a familiar interstate route. I didn't question or examine what happened but just thanked God once again.

In November 1994, I was really sick. I'd just finished another extremely exhausting week at work and had vowed to sleep late on Saturday morning. When I tried to sit up to get out of bed, I felt very weak and nauseous. So weak and debilitated, in fact, that I had to crawl to the bathroom to get a glass of water. It was one of the few times I was pleased to live in such a tiny apartment because the bathroom was only ten steps away. I knew I'd feel better after drinking some water.

As I slowly crawled to the bathroom, I regretted being single and alone. Many single people suffer alone when they're sick. Although we love our freedom, it's the one drawback in our independent lifestyle. I hoisted myself up to the sink and used my cupped hands to gulp down the water. Soon after, I found myself lying on the bathroom floor, just weak and faint. I closed my eyes to rest for a moment, only to realize I was sinking deeper and deeper down to a new place, a place I'd never visited before. A very dark, pitch black space. There weren't even thoughts in this place. I struggled to come back, but I was too tired and surrendered to the calm of the darkness.

With relief, I sank into the darkness and eventually saw a tiny yellow dot further down the tunnel ahead of me that slowly grew larger and larger. Then I saw a crucifix and quickly realized I was in the famous tunnel. I was seeing the light at the end of the tunnel. My soul awakened and realized that a decision was needed at this juncture. I remember saying, "It's not time for me to go yet. I'm not finished." With those words, I slowly, slowly pulled back, feeling the cold tiles on the floor of the bathroom.

I crawled to the phone and called my friend Kyle. I explained to him I was feeling horribly sick. He told me to contact my doctor to get a prescription and that he would pick it up and deliver it to me. I called my doctor and described the symptoms. He diagnosed severe dehydration and immediately wrote a prescription for two huge pills. Within a couple of days, I was back to my busy schedule, feeling great, although I did start to drink more water. A lot more water.

In 1995, I decided to enroll in graduate school to achieve a doctoral degree. I loved learning and figured this would be a constructive and fulfilling experience. I used loans and tax refunds to pay for school, and I studied on the weekends, evenings and during the holidays. For eight years, I plodded along. It was exhausting because I decided to remain full-time on the job, for I didn't want to miss out on any career advancement opportunities at my federal agency.

One of my lowest points during my doctoral program occurred in early January, 2004, when I was unable to get in touch with my advisor. I had needed some guidance and support in developing my research sample. After repeated attempts to connect with him, I started to feel abandoned.

After reading my emails to search for his response, again I found nothing from him. That night I lay in bed, crying and pleading to God: "Please help me because I don't know where to turn or what to do next. None of my friends can help me because they don't understand the academic culture or my emotional state. I really want to finish this work. I'm begging for Your support and direction." I prayed hard that night with all of my heart and felt as if God had heard me. My sleep felt good that night.

The next day I went downstairs to my office and made some flyers to solicit research sample participants. A fanatical determination consumed me and I printed about fifty flyers and ran upstairs to get dressed. It was a blustery January evening and I bundled up warmly with hat, scarf and gloves. I combed the neighborhood, knocking on the doors of strangers, requesting participants for my research sample. The people who greeted me at the door said either, "Good luck," or, "No, I don't know of anyone." When I depleted my small stack of flyers, I went back home and printed some more. I remember exclaiming aloud, "I'm going to finish this degree with or without my advisor!"

Eighteen months later, after being immersed in my renewed persistence and determination, I had a fateful meeting with my advisor. He told me I was ready to defend my research study and even complimented me on my Methodology chapter (the research sample process). During my doctoral defense in July 2005, he told me he was proud of me. I was proud of me, too, and knew I had not done it alone. That I had God's help and help from my Angels.

Where Church Resides

I discussed in an earlier chapter some of my feelings about church. A church is just a building—a house, a cathedral, a temple, a mosque or a synagogue. The church is where our Higher Power resides. Each person finds God for him or herself, wherever that may be. I find God in everyday actions, places, and feelings. God is present in a kind action, like letting others merge ahead of you on the highway or giving a stranger some extra change when they run out of money for a purchase at the register. God is in a dewy morning with grass that glistens from a hard night's rain. God is in that one small voice that asks the school bully to stop hitting other kids. He is also in that person who protects animals from cruel people. And God is in me. I shine in his light.

God is everywhere and we are all connected to Him, sharing in the Divine Power. I wish we would all recognize this and stop believing that God is up there, outside of us, a separate entity. This passive approach to our own Divinity and capabilities must be challenged. We must take action and begin to create our own fulfilling lives, full of prosperity, abundance and peace. When we self-actualize, we are allowing God to use us as His instrument to do good things. We have one life to get it right. What is your contribution? How are you making the world a better place by demonstrating the God in you? We need responsible fathers, loving mothers and honorable leaders. Claim your Divine Power.

Healing From Animals

"Until You Have Loved an Animal, Part of Your Soul Remains Unawakened"

Throughout my healing journey, I have always had a pet—bunnies, turtles, love birds, fish, dogs, and I currently have five cats and a beta fish. I would like to have many more pets, but I do not have the additional time needed to care for them properly. There always seems to be just one more cat or dog to adopt, because people do not spay or neuter their pets. I wish people would read and learn about a pet before buying or adopting one. I know that at Easter time, bunnies look so cute, and on Christmas Day, it's fun to see a puppy jump out of a box. But having a pet is a 24/7 job, and animals need daily care and attention, not just on holidays. If you don't have your own act together, do not bring a sweet, innocent animal into your home. They deserve to live with healthy, kind people.

I love animals and I love caring for them. They have taught me a lot about myself because they mirror back to you what you show them. My cats have taught me to demand fair and dignified treatment from others and ignore me when I try to command or direct them harshly. They respond to kindness and gentleness, and their pure spirits and innocence communicate with my soul. In their presence, I am encouraged to maintain a joyful spirit.

I have loved turtles because they have a protective shell around them, into which they can retreat when they feel unsafe or threatened. With their prehistoric appearance, turtles have withstood the test of time.

I also love birds because they seem to serve as a connection between the earth and the heavens. They always seem to be happy, and spread their good cheer everywhere.

I appreciate reptiles, too, because they have thick skin, which is something I have tried to develop in myself. In a city like Washington, D.C., you need a thick skin because there are so many negative elements. Each one of God's creatures has taught me something about life, love, devotion and order.

Positive and Negative Energy

Through my healing process, I have been more keenly aware of positive and negative energy. As an empathic person, I absorb and sense different energies very easily, wherever I go. Because of this heightened sensitivity, I work hard to maintain positive thoughts because I will attract to myself what I hold in my mind. I also ensure that my home environment is peaceful, calm and restorative. I keep frankincense, sandalwood and lavender incense in the house, which I burn every morning while I read my *Daily Word*. The incense has a calming, spiritual effect that helps to establish a nurturing environment. I listen to soft, peaceful music to calm my spirit, and I avoid violent movies, loud people and chaotic environments.

I avoid negative people whenever possible because they lower my energy frequencies and attract negative outcomes. Negative energy can make you ill, attract negative outcomes and gradually debilitate the human body. I have seen this demonstrated in people who maintain negative attitudes. They are very often manifesting physical ailments of some kind, such as colds, allergies, strained muscles or are accident-prone. Mishaps always seem to accompany them.

Keeping positive thoughts in your head requires effort and discipline, and requires constantly being aware of your own thoughts and viewpoints. If this seems difficult for you, try a little exercise. Wear a rubber band on your wrist for the day and, whenever you catch yourself thinking a negative thought, snap the rubber ban on your wrist lightly. This will help you become more aware of your thoughts. Please practice this. With our positive thoughts, collectively we can change our homes, communities and eventually the world.

Using Your Subconscious Mind

Another way to keep positive thoughts in your mind is to think positive thoughts or read affirmations before going to sleep. You will be programming your subconscious mind, the part of your mind that continues to carry out bodily functions. The subconscious mind keeps your heart pumping, and performs digestion, breathing and other autonomous functions. It performs whatever we command of it, without reasoning or filtering what it receives. That is why it is never a good thing to have negative thoughts before retiring to bed. The subconscious mind acts on whatever we tell it.

The problem is that since birth, it also faithfully records everything that you see and hear. As an adult, we can mitigate what it records, but as children, there is no censorship, so whatever you are told is recorded. In my case, that was an unrelenting barrage of negativity that shaped my self-image for several decades. However, it can be "reprogrammed" by hypnosis or affirmations.

For many years, I listened to my self-help tapes before going to sleep. I listened to healing affirmations by Louise Hay and other positive tapes. This helped me erase the negative programming or self-limiting messages that I had learned over the years and were stored deep in my subconscious.

I really did learn how to "sleep on it," and whenever I had a complex problem to solve or a decision to make, I would tell my subconscious to work on that specific problem overnight while I slept. In the morning, upon awakening, I would always have a clear, solid answer or solution. I still often wake up with creative ideas and projects, many of which I have acted on with great success! The subconscious mind is greatly underutilized and we need to change this.

The Power of Forgiveness

I had to learn how to forgive. I couldn't just say it but had to feel it in my heart. Forgiveness requires the acknowledgement of Divine Love, and it takes a while to understand that. Rather than direct my anger and hatred towards men, it was more exciting and comforting to use it as fuel for my ambition. As long as I held onto the hatred for my ex-husband, the longer I was trapped in a negative relationship with him. I had to let him go to allow for other, more positive energies to enter into my life.

I eventually understood that the negative energies of hatred and anger were blocking the positive energy I needed to manifest my affirmations, goals and desires, so I had to reconcile my feelings toward him and lovingly release him and forgive him. When I really felt I had forgiven him, my life started to move in a positive direction.

The purpose that Doug had served in my life was revealed. In shaking off his control, I grew more strength, confidence, wisdom, and most importantly, my faith in God. I saw that Doug had been an instrument in God's plan for my life. Everything happens for a reason, and there are no accidental occurrences. My experience with Doug was an opportunity to get closer to God ... and I'm glad I did.

I believe that "problems" or disasters happen to remind us who is really in charge. We have so many opportunities to strengthen and renew our faith; some are gentle tugs, others are a kick in the butt, while others are life-threatening. It all depends on when you decide to listen for God, the Still Small Voice within each of us.

It took me about five years to forgive Doug. I told my mind, my heart and my spirit to forgive him, and began to envision him surrounded by God's love. As I lovingly released him, in my mind he became a sad, dysfunctional, misguided man who I just "happened" to encounter. In prayer, I thanked him for what he showed me about myself and how he had served as an instrument in God's plan. Then there was no more hatred towards him.

Months later, while walking home from a new job on a steamy hot July afternoon, a car pulled up alongside me. I stopped and quickly glanced at the driver. It was Doug. He smiled and asked, "You want a ride?" Without hesitation, I smiled, said, "Yes," and quickly got into his car without thinking. After buckling my seat belt, I started to panic on the inside from realizing what I had just done. I'd just stepped into the car of a man who had stalked me for over two years! I immediately thought that he might have a gun and that I could be dead in all of a minute. As he drove up 15th Street toward downtown, I remained calm and factual. Suddenly he blurted out, "Gina, let's get remarried!"

I gently told him, "We aren't compatible. I need you to drop me off at the next block."

He said he was sorry for the things he'd done and wanted us to try again. He promised that everything would be different this time. I thought to myself, "How many times have I heard *that* line?" I also didn't want him to have any ideas or details about where I was currently living, so I said again, "I need to get out right here."

He pulled over to the curb, and I told him to take care of himself as I quickly but calmly exited the car. I then walked *away* from my home. I rushed into a nearby coffee shop, found an empty table in the back, and sat down to control my shaking. I had let my guard down and could have been killed! I had totally forgiven him and his monstrous behaviors but vowed to never let my guard down again. I never saw him again after that encounter. I wish him well, wherever he is but I'm glad he's out of my life.

Once I had learned about the divinity in each of us, it became easier to forgive. I even worked through my negative emotions toward all Black men. I even wrote a poem about them:

To A Black Man
Hold me like tomorrow, touch me for today.
Know that in your sorrow, I'll not be far away.
Cry with all your passion, heal your secret sorrows.
Bathe your heart with tenderness, let only love build your tomorrow.
Deep within each cell, lie the memories full of pain.
Never to be forgotten, never for your gain.
Wishing to erase them, wanting to start anew,
Trapped inside the memories, trapped inside of you.
Cry with all your passion, heal your secret sorrows.
Bathe your heart with tenderness, because only love will build tomorrow.
With all my love, Gina.
© Gina Myers

I also finally forgave my Mom for leaving us. On every Mother's Day, I felt the loss. Finally, I was able to release and love her, believing she was still with me in some way. I honor her by accepting how much I am like her. We are similar souls and I see her in my achievements, actions, and ideas and will never forget her. I wrote:

I Haven't Forgotten
I pretend that you're gone, that you never were,
as Mother's Day approaches.
I ignore the soft rushing images of your love.
Your hands, your eyes — only to search for another's.
I pretend that I never belonged to you, as I search to belong
Somewhere, with someone.
I lost you.
And every Mother's Day reminds me
Of the big gaping hole from where you were.
I haven't forgotten you.
You play in my dreams.

You dance in my heart.
You glisten in my tears.
You remember the little girl that I once was.
That I still am.
And on every Mother's Day, I am reminded of your spirit,
As I
Try to pretend,
Try to ignore,
That you ever were.
Nola, I haven't forgotten.
© 2001 Gina Myers

Dad

I want to thank my Dad. I have long forgiven him for any harm I felt he inflicted upon me. I was an impressionable and sensitive child, growing up in a troubled environment, and he did the best he could. He was always there for us. He may not have been in the best mood all of the time, but he was there, not hanging out in the street or chasing women like a lot of men. He was a loyal and devoted husband who worked very hard at all kinds of jobs to put food on the table. He is a special spirit.

I remember at the age of seven, I had the joyous opportunity to tag along with him at work when he was a janitor at the Seaboard Office Building. I remember how he washed and scrubbed the toilets, whistling as he worked with a pride and efficiency that awed me. Most of all, I remember having him all to myself.

My Dad is unique. As a child, I watched him as he walked around the house doing chores on Saturday mornings, whistling or singing a song by Mario Lanza. He would belt out *"Beloved, the very stars above you are jealous of the way your eyes sparkle and shine!"* I still love that song to this day. He would also recite poetry at home. He loved poetry and would read it to Mama often. During really hard financial times when he was not sure how we were going to make it through tomorrow, he would make each of us recite:

*"Lead kindly light, keep thou
my feet. I ask not to see the
distant scene, one step is
enough for me."*

As a gifted and ingenious man, he would tackle almost any new task, believing he could do it. He could repair anything around the house, was a great cook, and even built a pond in our back yard for the ducks to swim in. He was great with first aid and would perform minor operations on the ducks, the dog or birds when necessary. He would have been a great surgeon.

When he got fed up from being laid-off so often from new jobs, he started his own painting company, which lasted until he obtained a steady job at Penelec. He was a superb painter and electrical technician. Once he obtained that decent paying job, he would never, ever take a day off from work unless it was for a dire emergency. Every single day, he was out of bed and reporting to work by 6:00 am, or whenever he was needed on a work shift. He loved his job and quickly learned how to deal with the few mean co-workers.

His consistent routine of getting up to go to work every single day at 6:00 in the morning taught us diligence and a great work ethic. It was also comforting to hear him whistling happily in the early morning, as he grabbed his lunch and uniform. He was happy to be working.

As I got older, I began to see my Dad as a distinct person and not as the stern authoritative figure I had dreaded. I began to look deeper at what made him the way he was and wondered how he had managed to survive. Through his family members and other siblings, I learned about his awfully painful childhood and the mental cruelties he had to endure. I soon realized how special he was and how I wanted to love him, not hate him. My admiration for him grew stronger.

I began to recall that, in spite of his misery about his early job struggles, he still tried to do what he could for all of us that would make us happy. He was focused on how we could develop and broaden our minds and outlook, and learn to appreciate the world outside the housing projects. We would take frequent drives out to the country to escape the drab life of the housing projects and day trips to nearby museums and zoos, just to experience new situations. Dad loved a parade and every holiday, he rounded us all up to go and get a prime seat to watch the parade. I often wondered why he loved parades so much. I can ask him.

He really loved animals and instructed us to love them and care for them. He allowed each of us to have a pet and we learned about the daily responsibility of taking care of them. He said, "They are God's creatures and are kinder and more civil than man." He went out of his way to adopt and protect all kinds of animals. We would often go to the Erie Zoo during the winter to visit the buffalo, especially one huge buffalo that we fed apples to. After several apples, that buffalo did a happy shuffling of his feet, which Dad loved. He also loved watching it move quickly on its feet, like Fred Astaire.

Dad could grow any kind of flower or tree, and we learned how to appreciate nature and care for flowers. He always had beautiful flowers in our yard and he meticulously maintained our lawn. Even while we were living in the projects, we had a sand box in the yard and grew huge sunflowers.

He enjoyed caring for plants and the lawn. Early on Saturday mornings during the summer months, while we were all still asleep, he would go outside, unroll the hose, and sit on the front steps, watering the lawn. Sometimes, I'd quietly get out of bed and peep out of the window to watch him, in deep thought about something. He would be out there for almost an hour, thinking and sometimes whistling. Whenever I heard him whistling, I'd smile, knowing it was going to be a good day.

My Dad taught me a lot of good habits that helped me survive through hard times. He said, "Never quit," and hung a poster on the kitchen wall when we were kids. It read:

"Press On
Nothing in the world can take the place of persistence.
Talent will not. Nothing is more common than unsuccessful men with
talent.

Genius will not. Unrewarded genius is almost a proverb.
Education will not.
The world is full of educated derelicts.
Persistence and determination alone are omnipotent!"

I still keep a framed copy of that saying in my office. He taught us about being honest and forthright, and would always say, "Your word is your bond." I learned how to honor the words and promises I made to others, and could never understand how a person could commit to something and not follow through. I have often been disappointed by others whom I assumed were honorable with their words.

Dad had a lot of integrity and was always trying to do what was right. He also hated pettiness, stupidity and filth. He would always say, "Being poor is one thing, but you don't have to be poor and filthy."

He also taught us about safety. We teased him and called him "Safety Pete" because he was always teaching and reminding us about fire safety and how to handle life-threatening situations. He made it a mandate that all of us learn how to swim, stay physically active, and not lose our heads during an emergency. Instead of all the teasing we gave him, we should have given him a medal for his instruction and dedication. Through all the years, we never had any fire in our home from a space heater, candle or burning pot!

Most importantly, my Dad taught me how to overcome my fears and my shyness. He said, "Gina, don't let anyone tell you that you can't do something! They put on their pants the same way you do!" He often told me not to be shy and to speak up. His favorite saying to me was, "The squeaky wheel gets the grease!" I later remembered his statement and learned how to speak up with assertiveness in all types of settings.

My Dad has always practiced his religion but more recently, he has become a very spiritual man with a great reverence for God. He reads the Bible regularly and gains new insights from the familiar passages. He has become a gentler, wiser and more caring man. He demonstrates a mature honor towards women and has become more responsive to the concerns of others. Although he still has a temper, just like me, I am happy to say we are friends. We have both endured arduous journeys.

Dad also has an appreciation for angels, spirits and the unexplained. He has special gifts in this area and has had premonitions and forebodings. He is very broadminded about things in our world that science cannot explain or prove, and we have very unusual and exciting conversations on these topics.

On a deeper, more spiritual level, he is my Dad for a reason. I believe each of us is born into this world with a pre-determined mission. Long before our conception by our parents, our souls select our unique purpose and mission. We actually select who our parents will be as partners with us to fulfill our learning and our special Divine mission. I chose to be conceived by my parents. At that mystical intersection of timing and destiny, I became a soul enclosed in a physical body, ready to achieve my God-given mission. Through solitude and silence, it took me many years to learn about my Divine mission; and I thank my Dad for helping me to fulfill this mission.

Dynamics of Loving Relationships

My Dad always told me, "You have to love yourself first, before being able to give and receive real love from others." For a long time, however, I never understood what this meant but I think I've got it now. Simply put, people will treat you the way you treat yourself. If you believe you are worthless and act like it, they will respond accordingly. When you love yourself, you are capable of loving others unconditionally. Your self-image does not depend on their positive or negative actions towards you or their opinion of you. You know who you are and you believe in your own value, so your God-given divinity stays intact.

If you believe you are worthy of love and attention from others, you will send out this energy and attract people to you who will support and care about you. I have several good, true friends and a wonderful stepmother, Rena, who I consider to be one of my best friends. She was patient during the process of building our relationship, and allowed me the space and time to see, understand and accept her as my stepmother. She has a loving, courageous and caring spirit, and will help anyone in need. I believe she is an angel here on earth.

There is a saying, "God sends angels down to earth to look after us, and we know them as friends." What I admire most about Rena is how she frequently talks with my Dad and helps him process the traumatic events in his life. She has really helped him and I love her for this. She always tries to do the right thing, which is perhaps one of the many reasons he was attracted to her. They are both very honorable people, dutiful and sensitive towards others, and I feel blessed by having Rena in my life. She really feels like my mother, and I confide in her and feel much loved by her.

I also have two wonderful friends, Don and Kevin, who taught me about "prosperity consciousness." I love these two chocolate brown brothers, who exude an aura of, "I expect the best and the best comes to me." I met them about ten years ago during a consulting project, and they both exude love, tenderness, nurturing and support. They allow me to be myself and accept all the facets of my personality, whether it's the little girl in me, the curious intellectual, the silly prankster or the mature professional.

They do not impose structure on our friendship or place expectations on me. However and whenever I choose to find them, to have a conversation or seek advice, they acknowledge me with love and understanding. They are my Washington, D.C. "brothers" and, during the holiday season, when I don't feel like traveling home, they are my Brothers away from home. I can show up at their door almost anytime and get a big hug. Don is an extraordinary chef, and his exquisite culinary skills continually amaze me and my tummy. I love sitting with him in the kitchen with a glass of wine, talking about life, while watching him work his magic. They both taught me about abundance, luxury and prosperity by exemplifying it.

I have a good girlfriend and kindred spirit named Dina. Both of us are special spirits. She has enough wisdom, compassion and strength for an army, but is also very sensitive and gentle, yet she tries to hide her gentleness. She truly is a supportive Black woman to whom I can pour my heart out and feel nurtured and blessed. She is an angel in disguise and I'm very glad she's my friend.

I have male friends who admire, honor and care about me. I appreciate how they are not threatened by my achievements or success, for it takes a really solid and secure man to appreciate an accomplished woman. I am grateful they are in my life and continue to teach me a lot about myself as our friendships evolve.

I have learned that friends meet you where you are on the road to your higher self. Some friendships end because the mutual growth and evolution stop. It's sad when it happens, but it's necessary for spiritual growth. New friends come into my life to help me move to the next higher level yet I love it when two friends continue to grow together, for that is truly a blessing.

Over the years, I've taken the time to develop my own descriptions of what constitutes a good relationship:

What Constitutes a Relationship?
(Or Being Under the "Human Love Umbrella")
- Sharing mutual expectations.
- Experiencing a level of comfort, latitude and freedom to be yourself.
- Exposing your vulnerabilities to each other and still feeling close and safe with each other.
- Demonstrating consistent behaviors that give truth to your expressed words.
- Taking care of each other, without a crippling dependency on each other.
- Expressing love and frequent affection without doubting that it is joyfully received.
- Learning how much to give of yourself, so that if it is not reciprocated, you do not feel eviscerated and empty.
- Being sensitive enough to know which words will help in a

situation or compassionately knowing that a touch is needed instead.

- Understanding the fierce damage of the past and being patiently attentive to help the other person unlearn the bad things.
- Noticing what puts a smile on the other person's face and secretly remembering what it was that put it there.
- Doing some things together and some things apart, and talking about the things you do apart, only to learn more about each other.
- Being naturally forthright, genuine and tactful in communicating with each other.
- Squashing ego games, power plays and manipulation with thoughtfulness and kindness.
- Knowing that you will still be loved when you stick up for yourself.
- Being silly and serious, almost always at the same time.
- Never feeling you're bugging the other person when you want affection or attention.
- Knowing that if some one leaves you, there will be many more eager to love you!

The process of developing these descriptions helped me clarify in my mind what was important to me in a relationship with a close friend or loved one. We each must decide for ourselves what type of relationship will be beneficial for us, addressing our personal desires and needs.

A Personal Change Process

Changing and adapting to a new situation is not easy. As I have presented in this book, it first starts with awareness. Something must serve as a "triggering event" or a series of triggering events, which eventually "opens our eyes." This moment or moments of awareness are very valuable, and it is during these that you must begin to reflect and sort out what you want to do with that new awareness. The choices are either to act or to do nothing. Not making a choice is the same thing as choosing to do nothing.

My choice to leave Doug occurred when I looked into the mirror and saw me. I listened to that Still Small Voice from within. With power from my own God-given spirit, I felt capable of making a monumental change in my life. It began with one small action—to decide.

To continue taking consistent action requires a strong belief in the desired change, a belief in your own ability to make the change happen, and an accurate assessment of the disciplined effort involved to be successful (see *A Personal Change Process Model* in Appendix 1). It is important to seek help to work through this process because an outside objective person such as a therapist, coach or mentor can help with the tasks of exploring your subconsciously learned beliefs, assessing the influence you feel you have in recreating your life, and helping you to reshape your desired future path. For more information about methods and suggestions to help you achieve this change, see my website at: www.drginamyers.com

Supportive positive friends, loved ones and a healthy environment will help maintain and reinforce the new path you have chosen. Friends and loved ones can serve the purpose of assisting and supporting your new intentions, behaviors and habits. Through their positive involvement in your life and their mutually shared ideas and positive conversations, they will help you create new possibilities for a more meaningful and prosperous life.

Most importantly, it is up to you to decide what you want to do with your life. This is not a dress rehearsal; this is your life. Your one chance to get it right. Choose to take action. You will succeed!

Onward and Upward!

"Life shrinks or expands in proportion to one's courage."
— *Anais Nin*

I hope that this little book has helped someone. I have shared my own personal story about my life, full of adventure, excitement, love, sadness and domestic violence. I know how much effort and intention is needed to change your life. It is very difficult to leave someone who had appeared to love you so deeply. It's been said that it's easier to stay in an abusive, violent situation than it is to leave it because at least you know it. You know the drama, the mood swings, the periodic beatings, the heightened anxiety and the constant focus on avoiding danger. You already know the victim response. You have been convinced and brainwashed that you are incapable of handling life without your abuser. But you are capable. God knows you are.

Have faith and develop the courage. When I finally left my abusive husband, I was forced to create my own life, my own healthy relationships and my own reason for being. I had to leave the comfortable victim role and figure out how to manage my change process, a process that felt awkward, incomplete, risky and full of uncertainty.

Once you decide to change your life for the better, you'll discover there is so much help out there. There are many social services available in your own city, with people who care and are very eager to support and assist you on your new path. You don't have to go through it alone. You will make new friends and meet many "angels" who will help you along the way. Angels of all races, religions, and backgrounds. Be open to their assistance.

Believe in possibilities! Muster your courage to begin working on a plan. Choose to be in life, not sitting on the side, watching others achieve their happiness. If you are in touch with your feelings, life will continue to be very dynamic, full of the happy elated peaks and dismally low valleys. Without an anchor, it's easy to be steered off course. My faith is my anchor. My passionate love affair with God helps me navigate through troubles. I stay focused on the possibilities, not the problems. With determination, disciplined action and positive believing, your life will begin to change.

Using this approach, I have found I have more joy and energy. Through regular prayer, meditation and yoga, I stay in touch with my Divine mission—helping others. I have not had a depressing period for several years. Of course, I become disappointed and occasionally disillusioned but I work through it. I review my affirmations, I open my Bible, and I stop to talk with my Maker.

My life is good; I am very thankful for it. Through daily awareness, I am finally reaching a balance between my mind, body and spirit. I have learned to honor myself and take care of myself through proper nutrition, relaxation, fun activities and a peaceful home environment. Peacefulness starts inside. It all starts at home or wherever your sanctuary exists. When I am troubled by life's mishaps, I remember the phrase: *"Be still and know that I am God."* In the quiet solitude, I am reminded of who I really am and why I am here.

I have shared a lot with you and hope I have helped you. I want to continue to honor God by helping others, because God continues to help me. When I see the news about women being set on fire or shot by their husbands, I realize it could have been me. I was protected and saved for a reason.

I shall help enlighten and embrace other women and perhaps men, who may be misguided and feeling lost and alone. I must let them know that the Divine Power is in each of us!

A Personal Change Process Model

(adapted from Kolb 1996 & Ajzen 1993)

Keys: Awareness, Learned Beliefs, Reflection, Choice, Action, and Discipline as the Focal Point.

Without discipline, all intention and effort for positive personal change is lost. Discipline drives the entire process for a renewed life. It is the glue that creates a changed life filled with promise, success, and peace. Without discipline, all energy expended is consumed and scattered by the next distraction, leaving nothing accomplished at the end of the day, at the completion of a week, and upon the reflection of a life.

Dr. Gina Myers ©2006

Appendix 1: Bibliography

A Course in Miracles: Foundation for Inner Peace. Tiburon, CA. 1975/1985

Age, Mark. 1970. *How to Do All Things: Your Use of Divine Power.* Florida: Mark-Age Meta-Center, 1970.

Applegate, Liz. 2001. *Eat Smart, Play Hard.* New York: St. Martin's Press.

Beattie, Melody. 1987. *CoDependent No More!*

Bourne, Edmund, J., *The Anxiety and Phobia Workbook.* (Date & publisher unavailable.)

Bristol, Claude M., 1948. *The Magic of Believing.* New York: Simon & Schuster.

Bryan, Mark. 1999. *Codes of Love: How to Rethink Your Family and Remake Your Life.* New York: Simon & Schuster, Inc.

Budenz, Daniel, T. 1990. *The Caring Persons Illness: Codependency/The Affected Family Disease.* Minnesota: CompCare Publishers.

Carter, Steven, & Sokol, Julia. 1996. *Men Like Women Who Like Themselves.* New York:Dell Publishing Group, Inc.

Chopra, Deepak. 1993. *Creating Affluence: The A-to-Z Steps to a Richer Life.* San Rafael, CA: Amber-Allen Publishing.

Crary, Robert, Wall. 1987. *The Still Small Voice.* Ohio: Rishis Institute of Metaphysics.

Crary, Robert, Wall, 1996. *The Voice From Within.* Ohio: Rishis Institute of Metaphysics.

Cohen, Alan, 1987. *Dare to Be Yourself: How to Quit Being an Extra in Other People's Movies and Become the Star of Your Own.* Alan Cohen Publications.

Copeland, Mary Ellen. 1992. *The Depression Workbook: A Guide for Living With Depression and Manic Depression.* CA: New Harbinger Publications, Inc.

Curtis, Brent & Eldredge, John. 1997. *The Sacred Romance: Drawing Closer to the Heart of God.* TN: Thomas Nelson Publishers.

Eadie, Betty. 1992. *Embraced by the Light.* Placerville, CA: Gold Leaf Press.

Edelman, Hope. 1994. *Motherless Daughters: The Legacy of Loss.* New York: Dell Publishing.

Fedders, Charlotte; Elliot, Laura. 1987. *Shattered Dreams.* New York: Harper & Row Publishers.

Fisher, Antwone. 2001. *Finding Fish.* New York: HarperCollins Publisher, Inc.

Gawain, Shakti. 1991. *Awakening: A Daily Guide to Conscious Living.* CA: New World Library.

Goleman, Daniel & Bennet-Goleman, Tara. 1986. *The Relaxed Body Book*. New York: Doubleday & Company.

Graham, Dee, L. 1994. *Loving to Survive: Sexual Terror, Men's Violence and Women's Lives*. New York: New York University Press.

Gravitz, Herbert. 1998. *Obsessive Compulsive Disorder: New Help for the Family*. CA: Healing Visions Press.

Gray, John. 1992. *Men Are From Mars, Women Are From Venus*. New York: Harper Collins Publishers, Inc.

Gray, John. 1992. *Mars and Venus: The Languages of Love*. New York: HarperCollins Publishers, Inc.

Hanh, Nhat, Thich. 1975. *The Miracle of Mindfulness: A Manual on Meditation*. Boston: Beacon Press.

Hendrix, Harville. 1988. *Getting the Love You Want: A Guide for Couples*. New York: Harper & Row Publishers.

Kaufman, Gershen. 1992. *Shame: The Power of Caring*. Rochester, Vermont: Schenkman Books, Inc.

Kingma, Daphne, Rose. 1991. *True Love: How to Make Your Relationship Sweeter, Deeper and More Passionate*. ME: Conari Press.

Knowles, Malcolm. 1990. *The Adult Learner: A Neglected Species*. Houston, Texas: Gulf Publishing Company.

La Berge, Stephen. 1985. *Lucid Dreaming: The Power of Being Awake and Aware in Your Dreams*, New York: Balantine Books.

Lama, Dalia & Cutler, Howard, 1998. *The Art of Happiness: A Handbook for Living*. New York: Riverhead Books, Penguin Putnam, Inc.

Leonard, George. 1991. *Mastery. The Keys to Success and Long-Term Fulfillment*. New York: Penguin Books.

Lorr, Regina & Crary, Robert. 1983. *The Path of Light*. Marina del Rey, CA: DeVorss & Company P.O. Box 550.

Martin, Del. 1983. *Battered Wives*. New York: Simon & Schuster.

Matsakis, Aphrodite. 1997. *Trust After Trauma: A Guide to Relationships for Survivors and Those Who Love Them*. (p.62) Oakland, CA: New Harbinger Publications, Inc.

McGinnis, Alan, Loy. 1990. *The Power of Optimism*. New York: HarperCollins Publishers, Inc.

McKenna, Christine, A. 1992. *Love, Infidelity, and Sexual Addiction: A Codependent's Perspective*. IN: Abbey Press.

Murphy, Joseph. 1963. *The Power of Your Subconscious Mind*. New Jersey: Prentice Hall, Inc.

Murphy, Joseph. 2001. *The Amazing Laws of Cosmic Mind Power*. New York: Prentice Hall Press, Inc.

Niven, David. 2000. *The 100 Simple Secrets of Happy People*. CA: HarperCollins Publishers, Inc.

Parker, Alice, Anne. 1991. *Understand Your Dreams: 1,001 Basic Dream Images and How to Interpret Them*, CA: H. J. Kramer, Inc.

Robbins, Jhan, & Fisher, David. 1972. *Tranquility without Pills: All About Trancendental Meditation*. New York: Peter H. Wyden, Inc. Publisher.

Roman, Sanaya. 1989. *Spiritual Growth: Being Your Higher Self*. CA: H.J. Kramer, Inc.

Roman, Sanaya. 1986. *Personal Power Through Awareness: A Guidebook for Sensitive People*. CA: H. J. Kramer, Inc.

Ross, Ruth. 1982. *Prospering Woman: A Complete Guide to Achieving the Full, Abundant Life*. New York: Bantam Books.

Russell, Kathy; Wilson, Midge, & Hall, Ronald. 1992. *The Color Complex: The Politics Of Skin Color Among African Americans*. New York: First Anchor Books, Random House.

Ruzek, Joe. 2006. *"Coping With PTSD: Coping with PTSD and Recommended Lifestyle Changes for PTSD Patients"*. National Center for PTSD, United States Department of Veterans Affairs. www.ncptsd.va.gov/facts/treatment/fs_coping.html

Shengold, Leonard. 1989. *Soul Murder: The Effects of Childhood Abuse and Deprivation,* New York: Ballantine Books.

Shain, Merle. 1989. *Courage My Love: A Book to Light an Honest Path*. New York: Bantam Books.

Sills, Judith. 1987. *A Fine Romance: The Psychology of Successful Courtship – Making It Work For You*. New York: St. Martin's Press.

Stahl, Louann. 1992. *A Most Surprising Song: Exploring the Mystical Experience*. St. Louis, Missouri: Unity Books.

Sternberg, Robert. 1987. *The Triangle of Love: Intimacy, Passion, Commitment*. New York Basic Books, Inc. Publishers.

Thoele, Sue Patton.1992. *The Woman's Book of Confidence- Meditations for Strength And Inspiration,* New York: MJF Books.

Thoele, Sue, Patton. 1991. *The Woman's Book of Courage: Meditations for Empowerment and Peace of Mind*. CA: Conari Press.

Turner, Tina. 1986. *I, Tina*. New York: Avon Books.

Virtue, Doreen. 1999. *Healing With the Angels: How Angels Can Assist You In Every Area of Your Life,* CA: Hay House, Inc.

Woodson, Carter, G. 1933. *The Mis-Education of the Negro*. Washington, D.C.: The Associated Publishers.

CPSIA information can be obtained at www.ICGtesting.com
Printed in the USA
BVOW082222160912

300448BV00006B/5/A